*Stagnation and the Financial Explosion*

# *Stagnation and the Financial Explosion*

Harry Magdoff
and
Paul M. Sweezy

AAKAR

Stagnation and the Financial Explosion
*Harry Magdoff and Paul M. Sweezy*



First Published in India 2008
**Reprinted 2020**

ISBN 978-81-89833-40-4

Published in agreement with Monthly Review Press, New York for South Asia.



*Published by*
**AAKAR BOOKS**
28 E Pocket IV, Mayur Vihar Phase I
Delhi 110 091, India
www.aakarbooks.com

*Printed at*
Sapra Brothers, Noida

# *Contents*

# *Introduction*

In the "Afterword to the Second German Edition" of *Das Kapital* Marx called attention to an aspect of the history of economic thought in the nineteenth century which, though in an entirely different context, has had a striking analogue in our time. The period from 1820 to 1830, he wrote, was notable in

> England for scientific activity in the domain of political economy. It was the time as well of the vulgarizing and extending of Ricardo's theory, as of the contest of that theory with the old school. Splendid tournaments were held.... The unprejudiced character of this polemic—although the theory of Ricardo already serves, in exceptional cases, as a weapon of attack on bourgeois economy—is explained by the circumstances of the time.... The literature of political economy in England at this time calls to mind the stormy forward movement in France after Dr. Quesnay's death, but only as a St. Martin's summer reminds us of spring. With the year 1830 came the decisive change.
>
> In France and in England the bourgeoisie had conquered political power. Thenceforth the class struggle, practically as well as theoretically, took on more and more outspoken forms. It sounded the knell of bourgeois economy.... It was thenceforth no longer a question whether this theorem or that was true, but whether it was useful to capital or harmful, expedient or inexpedient, politically dangerous or not. In place of disinterested inquirers there were hired prizefighters; in place of genuine scientific research, the bad conscience and the evil intent of apologetic.

Marx wrote this in 1872 at the dawn of the modern imperialist era and shortly after the defeat of the Paris Commune. The class struggle in the advanced capitalist countries entered a new phase, and so did bourgeois economics with the triumph of the marginal utility schools in Austria, France, and Britain in the early 1870s. There followed roughly a half century of relative social peace and complacent economic theorizing, climaxed by the "New Era" of Henry Ford and "endless prosperity."

Then came the Crash of 1929, the Great Depression, and the deepening stagnation of the 1930s. Social struggles, in both the international and class arenas, intensified. Mainstream economics was stunned and helpless. The threatened bourgeoisies of the advanced capitalist countries reacted in two ways, exemplified by Nazi Germany and New Deal America.

Under these circumstances, the need for a new theory to help account for what was happening and to show the way to remedial policies was obvious and urgent. John Maynard Keynes met the challenge. As the most prestigious member of the Cambridge school, he was in a position to be listened to; as a brilliant theorist with a deep instinct for the survival of both England and capitalism, he appreciated the gravity of the situation and the necessity to escape from the confines of traditional economic dogmas. The publication in 1936 of his *General Theory of Employment, Interest and Money* signalled a revolution in economic thought comparable to that wrought by Adam Smith and David Ricardo a century and a half earlier.

But no revolution is without its counter-revolution. The stalwarts of the economics profession, regrouping their battered forces, moved to expunge the Keynesian heresy; and what looked like developing into a "spendid tournament," reminiscent of those of the period 1820-30, soon began to fill the pages not only of the professional economic journals but also of the business press and even the popular media. The form of this polemic was determined by the events of 1937-38. A recovery from the Great Depression that followed the crash of 1929 began in 1933 and continued, slowly but without serious interruption, for the next four years. Unemployment declined from 25 to 15 percent of the labor force, and things seemed on the way back to normal. Then, in the summer of 1937, the sky fell in. A sharp recession pushed unemployment back up to 19 percent in a few months, with no sign of resumed progress to be seen. Suddenly not only the economics profession but the country as a whole was faced with a question that could no longer be ignored or evaded: *Full Recovery or Stagnation?** The government itself soon joined the fray with the appointment by President Roosevelt of a Temporary National Economic Committee (TNEC), perhaps the most elaborate official inquiry into the condition of the economy ever mounted in this or any other country. Well-publicized hearings with star witnesses were held, and literally dozens of monographic studies were commissioned.

But the whole enterprise was short-lived. Even before the TNEC could issue its anticlimactic report, attention shifted dramatically from the sputtering economy to the Second World War. War orders came pouring in from Britain and France, and the United States began its own build-up for entry into the conflict two years later. The concerns of the 1930s were put aside as the U.S. economy spurted forward: by 1944 the GNP had increased by more than three quarters, and unemployment had sunk to less than 2 percent of the labor force.

Memories of stagnation lingered on, however, and this became a significant force in restraining the exuberance of the aftermath boom that normally follows a destructive war. It was not until the 1950s that the business community was converted to a mood of long-run optimism that was to contribute in its turn to the prolongation of the upswing that characterized the early postwar decades. The economics profession was quicker to forget the past. The interrupted debate of the 1930s was never revived; and even the publication in 1952 of the most thorough and penetrating study ever made of the problem of stagnation—Josef Steindl's *Maturity and Stagnation in American Capitalism*—was hardly noticed in the scholarly journals here or abroad.

The virtual disappearance of practical and scientific interest in the extraordinary—and at the time totally unanticipated—events of the 1930s did not, however, signify any change

* This is the title of a collection of essays published in 1938 by Professor Alvin Hansen of Harvard, the most prominent of Keynes's followers on this side of the Atlantic and, along with Professor Joseph Schumpeter, also of Harvard, a leading protagonist in the developing polemic of the late 1930s.

in the underlying forces at work. In its innermost essence capitalism has always been a process of capital accumulation, and at no time in its history has this process been smooth or uninterrupted. This unevenness has been most evident and violent in the "normal" business cycle, universally recognized by all schools of economic thought. But it has manifested itself as well in longer waves of speeded-up and retarded growth. Until the 1930s, the interest of economists was mostly focused on the business cycle, with the longer waves only rarely being subjected to serious economic analysis. But what happened during that decade forced a recognition, at least for a brief time, that the cycle operates within the context of the longer waves, and that the latter also need to be analyzed and understood. Unfortunately, as related above, the effort to satisfy this need was cut short, and the economics profession generally reverted to its earlier stance of blocking out all but the short-term phenomena of the "normal" cycle.

This was, to put it mildly, the path of least resistance: no one who counted for anything—in business, in government, in academia—wanted to be reminded of the 1930s; and anyone who, like the present writers, kept insisting that, given the nature of the capitalist system, what had happened in the past not only could but almost certainly would happen again, was dismissed as hopelessly out of date and obviously incapable of understanding the "new economics" as preached by the high priests of the new capitalist faith.

It is true that for a while in the 1970s stagnation in the guise of "stagflation" crept back into the economists' (and the public's) consciousness. But there was little inclination to take it seriously, and nothing faintly resembling the deeply concerned debates of the late 1930s emerged. And when Ronald Reagan came along with his unique brand of "Voodoo" economics—the motto and guiding principle of which should be "après moi le deluge"—the ideologues of the ruling class, many of whom certainly knew better, distinguished themselves by hailing the great recovery of the 1980s and professing to believe that it marks but the beginning of a new golden era of economic expansion.

Now, in the late summer of 1986, reality is well on the way

to putting an end to this demeaning farce. The recovery that began at the end of 1982 has palpably run its course. As in the summer of 1937, when the upswing dating from 1933 suddenly collapsed, no restarting of the engine of capital accumulation is in prospect. The stimulatory medicine that Keynesian theory prescribes for depressions—massive doses of deficit spending—has already been used up. There is nothing left in the entire bag of tricks. The reality of stagnation on a scale not experienced for half a century now stares us in the face. It is high time for the Great Debate to be resumed.

We offer this book—the fourth in a series dating back to 1972—as a contribution to this crucially important enterprise.* Like its predecessors, it brings together essays originally published in *Monthly Review* that seek to analyze the current condition and direction of movement of the U.S. and global capitalist economies. Stagnation has of course been a recurrent—one might almost say ever-present—topic in these essays, and the purpose of this introduction so far has been to put this theme into meaningful, if all too sketchy, historical perspective. But long experience has taught us that there are other questions that need to be touched on in an introduction to a collection of this kind.

We both reached adulthood during the 1930s, and it was then that we received our initiation into the realities of capitalist economics and politics. For us economic stagnation in its most agonizing and pervasive form, including its far-reaching ramifications in every aspect of social life, was an overwhelming personal experience. We know what it is and what it can mean; we do not need elaborate definitions or explanations. But we have gradually learned, not altogether to our surprise of course, that younger people who grew up in the 1940s or later not only do not share but also do not understand these perceptions. The economic environment of the war and postwar periods that played such an important part in shaping their experiences was

---

* The earlier ones are *The Dynamics of U.S. Capitalism: Corporate Structure, Inflation, Credit, Gold, and the Dollar* (1972); *The End of Prosperity: The American Economy in the 1970s* (1977); *The Deepening Crisis of U.S. Capitalism* (1981).

very different. For them, stagnation tends to be a rather vague term, equivalent perhaps to a longer-than-usual recession but with no implication of possible grave political and international repercussions. Under these circumstances, they find it hard to relate to what they are likely to regard as our obsession with the problem of stagnation. They are not quite sure what we are talking about or what all the fuss is over.

There is a temptation to say: just wait and see, you'll find out soon enough. Indeed, this may be the only really satisfactory answer. Unless backed up by actual experience, explanations often mean little. And there is no doubt that what we see as indications of stagnation in the 1970s and 1980s are still a long way from the realities of half a century ago. But it would be a cop-out to leave it at that. We owe it to our readers at least to try to make clearer what we mean by stagnation and why we think it is so important.

It may be useful to begin with a quotation from an article in a recent issue of the *Journal of Post-Keynesian Economics.* In the half century ending in 1983, according to the authors,

> there have been only ten years (ignoring World War II and conversion) in which actual GNP has equaled or exceeded potential. Those ten years have been noteworthy for the presence of expansionary government. Unfortunately, most of the expansion was warladen. Three of those years (1950-52) were during the Korean War; five of them were during the Vietnam War, which overlapped the activist, Kennedy-Johnson, Keynesian, civilian expansionist regimes. Without the strong pull from government demand over the last half century, the civilian economy has achieved its potential only in 1956 and 1973. Even those two years, on the basis of the utilization of human resources (unemployment) criterion, were significantly inferior to 1929.*

Though hardly comparable to the gloomy performance of the 1930s, this record does clearly indicate that the forces that were then overwhelmingly dominant had by no means disappeared in the new postwar climate. What did change—and this

* John F. Walker and Harold G. Vatter, "Stagnation—Performance and Policy: A Comparison of the Depression Decade with 1973-1984," *Journal of Post Keynesian Economics,* Summer 1986, p. 525.

is a matter of crucial importance that economic theory has only begun to recognize and deal with—is the way the economy as a whole has adjusted to and been reshaped by the persistent tendency of society's utilization of productive resources to lag behind its huge and growing potential. Whereas in the earlier period this tendency worked itself out in a catastrophic collapse of production—during the 1930s as a whole, unemployment and utilization of productive capacity averaged 18 percent and 63 percent respectively—in the postwar period economic energies, instead of lying dormant, have increasingly been channelled into a variety of wasteful, parasitic, and generally unproductive uses. This has been an enormously complex process that is still very imperfectly understood (in fact, mainstream economics does not even recognize its existence); the point to be emphasized here is that far from having eliminated the stagnationist tendencies inherent in today's mature monopoly capitalist economy, this process has forced these tendencies to take on new forms and disguises. At the same time, it is necessary to emphasize that these changes in the *form* of stagnation do not mean that the possibility of a generalized collapse of the whole structure no longer exists. This is a "problematic" that has come increasingly to the fore in the last few years, as reflected in some of the more recent essays in this collection (see especially "The Financial Explosion"), and it is one that is very much in our minds as we write this introduction.

Among the forces counteracting the tendency to stagnation, none has been more important or less understood by economic analysts than the growth, beginning in the 1960s and rapidly gaining momentum after the severe recession of the mid-1970s, of the country's debt structure (government, corporate, and individual) at a pace far exceeding the sluggish expansion of the underlying "real" economy. The result has been the emergence of an unprecedentedly huge and fragile financial superstructure subject to stresses and strains that increasingly threaten the stability of the economy as a whole. This should become clearer as we present updated evidence on these developments.

The dramatic change in the role of debt is clearly revealed

*Chart 1*
*Outstanding Debt and Gross National Product*

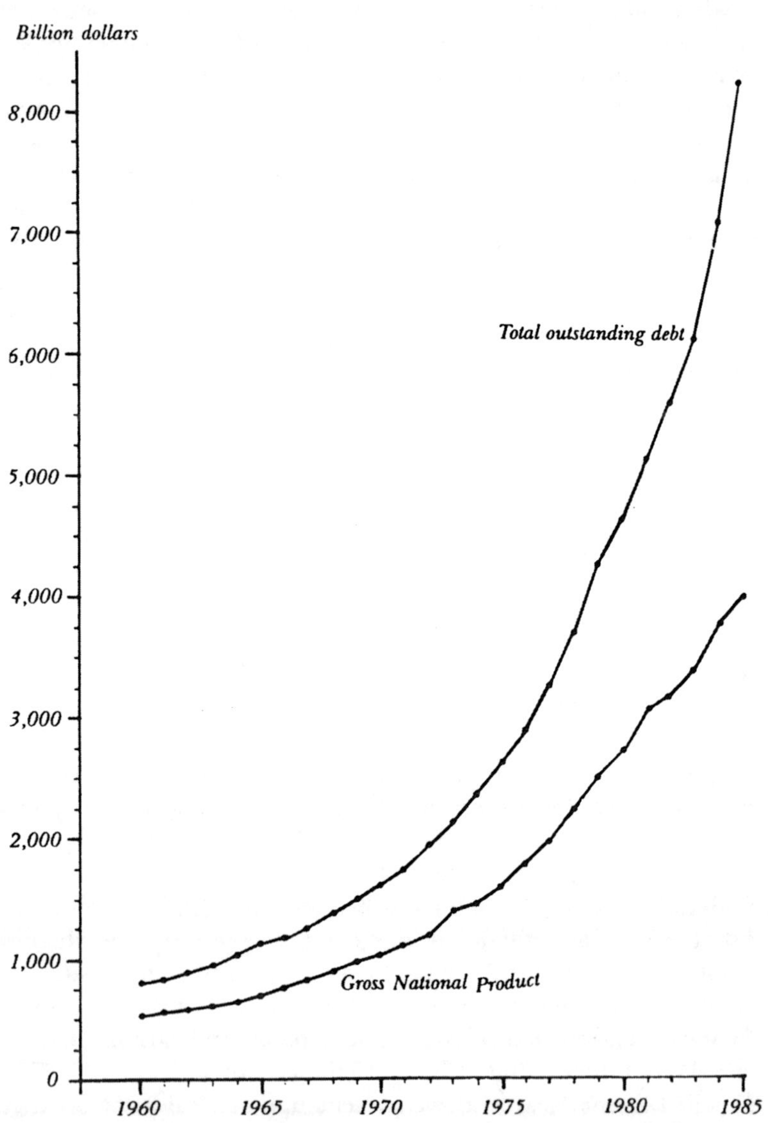


Source: Federal Reserve Board, *Flow of Funds Accounts* and *Survey of Current Business*, February 1986.

in Chart 1, which compares the total outstanding public and private debt with Gross National Product (GNP). Debt is of course a natural and necessary ingredient of a business economy. In the normal course of events, it grows in tandem with business activity, slowing down or declining during business downturns and expanding to fuel recoveries. And that was the way it went prior to the renewed onset of stagnation. Thus, the ratio of outstanding debt to GNP hovered around 1.5 between 1950 and 1960. But a change in the relationship had already begun to show up during the 1960s: debt started to accumulate at a somewhat faster rate than GNP. This can be seen in the widening of the gap between the two lines. A spectacular shift, however, became manifest in the 1970s: the more stagnation spread, the greater the reliance on debt as a prop to the economy. As can be seen from the chart, the gap between the two lines accelerated after 1970. Between 1970 and 1980, the ratio of debt to GNP advanced from 1.57 to 1.7. That, it turned out, was only a prelude to the debt explosion in the 1980s. By 1985, the total outstanding debt was twice as large as that year's GNP.

Especially significant is the way the increasing reliance on debt permeated every area of the economy. This can be seen in the growth patterns of debt in each of the four major components of the economy, presented in Table 1. The first line of the table includes state and local as well as federal indebtedness. In view of all the attention paid by the media and analysts to this area, it is useful to note that the rise in government borrowing was less than that of any of the other categories. In fact, government debt as a percent of the total declined from 34 percent in 1965 to 27 percent in 1985. What is particularly noteworthy, however, is that here as elsewhere debt dependency in the last fifteen years has been steadily increasing to compensate for a weakening private economy. Total government expenditures have been a major economic influence throughout the post-Second World War years, rising from 13 percent of GNP in 1950 to 20 percent in 1985. But while in the earlier years, surpluses in good years more or less balanced the deficits of recession periods, later on the pattern changed. Deficits began gradually to outweigh surpluses during the 1960s, and there-

*Table 1*
*Outstanding Debt*
*(Index numbers: 1965=100)*

| *Borrower* | *1965* | *1970* | *1975* | *1980* | *1985* |
|---|---|---|---|---|---|
| Government[a] | 100 | 123.1 | 182.4 | 284.5 | 585.8 |
| Consumers[b] | 100 | 140.1 | 226.8 | 421.2 | 696.5 |
| Nonfinancial business | 100 | 165.1 | 277.9 | 468.8 | 762.3 |
| Financial business | 100 | 200.5 | 421.6 | 917.0 | 1920.2 |
| Total | 100 | 144.6 | 236.5 | 414.4 | 742.4 |

Notes: a) Includes federal, state, and local governments.
b) This category is called "households" in the source of these statistics. Although consumers are the overwhelming component, the data also include personal trusts, nonprofit foundations, private schools and hospitals, labor unions, and churches.

*Source:* Federal Reserve Board, *Flow of Funds Accounts.*

after reliance on deficits rapidly increased. During the 1970s as a whole, deficits were needed to pay for 8 percent of federal government expenditures, whereas during the first half of the present decade this proportion more than doubled to 17 percent.

The rise in consumer debt shown in the second line of the table has been fostered by two factors: a strong desire to own homes and cars on the one hand, and an energetic promotion of lending by banks and finance companies on the other. Whenever the effective demand for these big-ticket items showed a tendency to taper off, lending terms were eased to widen the market. This practice was stimulated not only by manufacturers and house builders, but also by finance companies seeking a bigger share of this profitable business. But while this activity has propped up sales of homes and consumer durable goods, it has also piled up a mountain of consumer debt that is fast approaching an unsustainable limit: in 1970 the outstanding consumer debt amounted to about 68 percent of after-tax consumer income; in 1985 it was close to 85 percent.

As can be seen from line 3 of the table, nonfinancial business has been no stranger to the feverish accumulation of debt. The dominant component of this category of course consists of corporations, some of which have undertaken major debt obligations to keep alive, and are hence forced to keep on borrowing just to meet payments on past debt. Others, in contrast, have long been awash with idle cash, and many of these have also joined the parade. Unable to find profitable productive investment opportunities in the face of excess capacity and flagging demand, they have been eager participants in the merger, takeover, and leveraged buyout frenzy that has swept the country in recent years, becoming in the process both lenders and borrowers on an enormous scale. For all these reasons, nonfinancial corporations as a whole now carry a debt load of about $1.5 trillion, which, according to Felix Rohatyn, of the Lazard Frères investment banking firm, exceeds their total net worth by 12 percent. Moreover, Rohatyn points out, since 1982 the cost of servicing this debt has been absorbing 50 percent of the entire corporate cash flow. By comparison, during the 1976-79 recovery this cost averaged only 27 percent.*

But the most startling rate of growth in borrowing occurred in the financial sector itself (line 4 of Table 1). To a certain extent the numbers give an exaggerated impression of what actually happened. Since the debt of financial firms was relatively small in the base year, the rate of increase shows up as abnormally large when compared with the sectors that already had a much more substantial debt at the outset. Yet the transformation of the firms that are at the core of the debt explosion from minor to major borrowers is itself significant. Traditionally, most of these enterprises are intermediaries that receive otherwise idle funds, which are then lent out. But in the new financial environment, these firms have gone far beyond the role of intermediaries. They have themselves become large borrowers, thus stimulating a more rapid and intensive circulation of the economy's cash reserves.

Once started, this self-expansion of the financial sector has turned into a complex and enormously powerful process, with the most far-reaching consequences. The following summary of what has happened and the resulting changes in the financial picture is especially interesting in that it comes, as one might

* Felix G. Rohatyn in an address given before the Joint Economic Committee 40th Anniversary Symposium, Washington, D.C., January 16, 1986.

say, from the horse's mouth—the Federal Reserve Bank of New York:

> The volatility of prices for the entire spectrum of financial assets has risen considerably. In step with this development, new financial instruments—such as futures, options, and swaps—that provide additional ways to transfer price risks among market participants flourished. The active trading of these new instruments and of the more conventional instruments underlying them has burgeoned. The volume of financial transactions has accelerated at an unprecedented rate.
>
> Competition has greatly increased in the whole range of financial services. Commercial banks, thrift institutions, investment banks, and insurance companies are all expanding the range of their activities and crossing over into each other's traditional business preserves. Nonfinancial businesses are directly entering financial services as well. And foreign financial institutions are increasing their involvement in markets here at the same time that U.S. firms are expanding abroad. Competitive pressures have been compounded by the ongoing trend toward financial deregulation of the terms that institutions can charge or offer, the kinds of transactions in which they may engage, and the geographical markets they may enter. This increased degree of competition has squeezed earnings margins on many conventional financial activities, accelerating the development and diffusion of innovations.
>
> The weakened economic and financial condition of major sectors—energy, agriculture, commercial real estate, and various developing countries—has diminished the credit standing of many borrowers. One consequence has been that in recent years the costs of capital and funding for some bank lenders to those sectors have tended to rise relative to the costs for high quality commercial credits. At the same time, the direct credit markets have become more accessible to business borrowers. Banks have had a difficult time competing with the commercial paper and securities markets for corporate credit demands, especially those of the "blue chip" firms. Indeed, in many cases, banks have sought to profit from the trend toward market financing by generating loans and selling them off, either directly or packaged as securities, or by expanding their roles as guarantors and distributors of capital market instruments.
>
> All these forces—innovation, competition, deregulation, securitization, and the growth of trading—have combined to create a challenging environment.*

---

* Edward J. Frydl, vice-president and assistant director of research, "The Challenge of Financial Change," Federal Bank of New York, *Annual Report*, 1985.

The fact that the essay from which this passage comes constitutes the bulk of the latest annual report of the New York Federal Reserve Bank is of special significance. In the past these annual reports have been rather humdrum summaries of business and banking developments in the preceding year. The decision to depart from tradition was made, according to the Bank's president, because "the rapid transformations in the markets are unprecedented in their scope." In fact, there can be little doubt that the real reason was not to supply information but rather to press the alarm button. The essay starts off by noting that "extraordinary economic imbalances and financial strains have marked the course of the recovery." Although most of the danger spots are only gently hinted at, one specific reference to a potential disaster area boggles the mind:

> And last November a major clearing bank for securities transactions experienced a severe computer problem that could not be put right before closing. As a consequence, this Bank extended a record $22.6 billion loan on an overnight basis.
>
> That incident was well-contained and did not threaten to spill over to other institutions or markets. The computer difficulties were resolved the next day. But it dramatically points out the types of risks we face. Settlement disrupts stemming from more protracted operational problems may not be so limited in their consequences. And, of course, a settlement failure stemming from a default could play havoc throughout the financial system.

The possibility of settlement failures is only one of the areas of financial fragility, all of which, as the above quote implies, are parts of an extensive worldwide network of financial operations. Consciousness of this is what lies behind the warning, issued more recently by William Seidman, chairman of the Federal Deposit Insurance Corporation:

> The financial area is probably, next to nuclear war, the kind of area that can get out of control, and once out of control cannot be contained and will probably do more to upset the civilized world than about anything you can think of.*

Aware as the monetary authorities may be of the dangers that lie ahead, their hands are nonetheless tied. And the reason

* Cited in the *Financial Times*, 29 May 1986. It should come as no surprise that a banker equates the "civilized world" with capitalism.

is precisely the fragility of the system. Interference by the government or the monetary authorities, other than efforts to put out fires when they flare up, carries with it the potential of setting off a chain reaction. This explains why at every critical juncture existing restraints on further financial expansion have been relaxed in order to avoid a major breakdown. The removal of controls has in turn opened the door to still more innovations that add to the fragility.

What is especially striking in the present situation is that the more the financial system has moved away from its role as facilitator of the production and distribution of goods and services, the more it has taken on a life of its own, a fact that can be seen most vividly in the mushrooming of speculative activity, which is closely tied in with the debt explosion of the last ten years, as well as with the day-to-day-operations of financial firms. Felix Rohatyn, an acute observer of the financial scene, claimed in the talk cited above that today we have the "most unfettered speculation seen in this country since 1929." One indication of this is the jump in the average number of shares of stock traded *daily* on the New York Stock Exchange, from 19 million in 1975 to 109 million in 1985. Even more striking is the way the futures markets have come to dominate gambling activities. Back in 1960, futures contracts related almost entirely to commodities: in that year only 3.9 million contracts were written. This activity grew to 11.2 million in 1970, which was still within reason, given the growth in the economy. But the 1970s were a different story: by the middle of that decade, futures markets had been established in precious metals, foreign currency, and financial instruments. Other innovations followed (betting on the future of average stock prices, for example), and the dam burst. In 1980 over 92 million futures contracts were traded, in 1985 almost 160 million, with still no end in sight. This has become a major "growth industry" in the United States and is fast spreading to other major capitalist centers abroad.

Chart 2, comparing an index of the volume of futures trading with the Federal Reserve Board's index of industrial production, presents a graphic picture of this speculative explosion. Prior to 1970, futures trading grew at roughly the same pace as production. But then the economic slowdown of the 1970s set in, and production lagged while speculation skyrocketed. Since 1977, industrial production has increased 25 percent, the volume of futures trading by 370 percent! It is little wonder that *Business Week* (16 September 1985) editorialized: "Slow growth and today's rampant speculative binge are locked in some kind of symbiotic embrace."

Acknowledgment of this "symbiotic embrace," however, leaves open the question of which is cause and which effect. A popular line of thought places the blame on speculation (including the hectic buying and selling of corporations) as the cause of the country's industrial malaise. But for the diversion of funds to these wasteful activities, the argument holds, capital would be flowing into useful productive investment. On the other hand, Henry Kaufman, Managing Director of the Salomon Brothers investment banking firm and one of Wall Street's most astute analysts, sees it just the other way around: "The rapid expansion in bank reserves against a sluggish economic backdrop yielded the classic result: funds sought financial assets, given that there was no need to finance real economic activity."*

Kaufman's view is clearly the realistic one. It should be obvious that capitalists will not invest in additional capacity when their factories and mines are already able to produce more than the market can absorb. Excess capacity emerged in one industry after another long before the extraordinary surge of speculation and finance in the 1970s, and this was true not only in the United States but throughout the advanced capitalist world. The shift in emphasis from industrial to pecuniary pursuits is equally international in scope.

The growing relative importance of "making money," as distinct from "making goods," in the U.S. economy is highlighted in Table 2. The first column presents the dollar amounts of GNP accounted for by industries engaged in producing and shipping goods (agriculture, mining, construction, manufacturing, transportation, and public utilities) in selected years from 1950 to 1985. The second column gives the dollar amounts of

* Henry Kaufman, "In the Shadow of Financial Exhilaration," *Challenge*, July-August 1986.

*Chart 2*
*Speculation vs. Production*

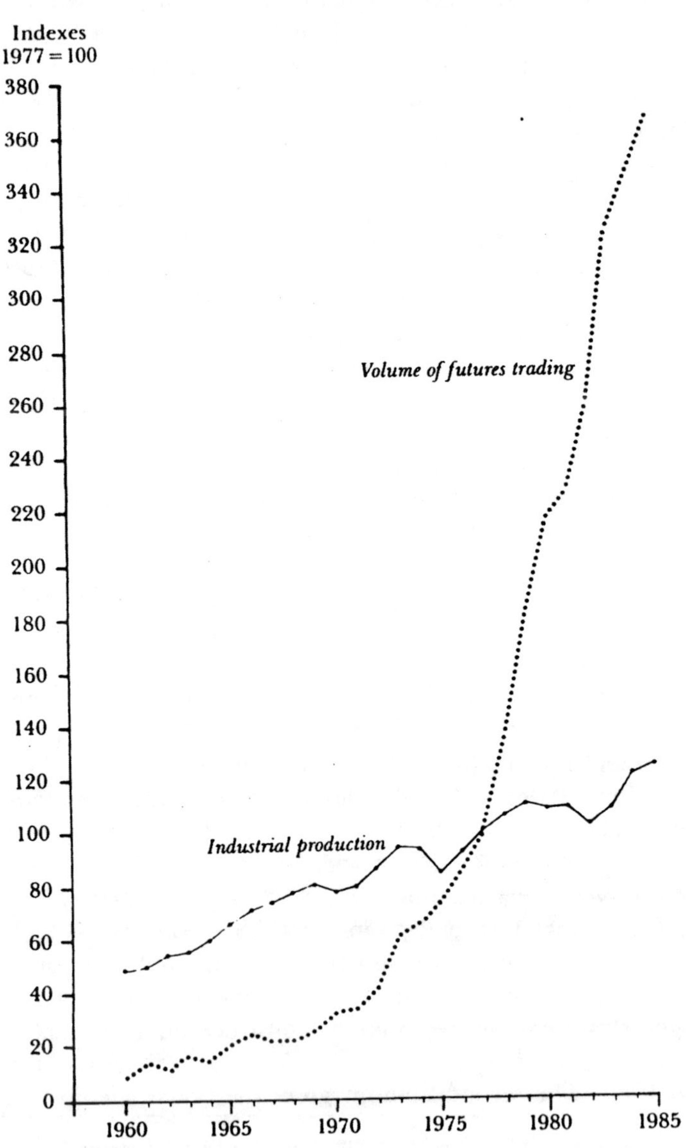


Source: Futures Trading Association and Federal Reserve Board.

*Table 2*
*Growth of the Financial Sector*

| | Gross National Product | | Financial sector |
|---|---|---|---|
| | Goods production[a] | Financial firms[b] | as a percent of goods production |
| | — Billions of dollars — | | |
| 1950 | 153.3 | 32.2 | 21.0 |
| 1960 | 250.5 | 72.8 | 29.1 |
| 1970 | 440.7 | 145.8 | 33.1 |
| 1980 | 1144.6 | 400.6 | 35.0 |
| 1985 | 1566.7 | 626.1 | 40.0 |

Notes: a) Agriculture, mining, construction, manufacturing, transportation, and public utilities.
b) Banks, other finance companies, real estate, and insurance.

*Source:* National income and product accounts, as reported in *Survey of Current Business,* various issues.

GNP attributed to the financial sector (finance, real estate, and insurance) in the same years. As can be seen, in 1950 the financial sector's contribution to GNP was 21 percent that of the goods sector; by 1985 this had almost doubled to 40 percent. Without doubt this reflects a structural change of unprecedented magnitude.

At this point we would do well to pause and reflect on the larger meaning of the dramatic developments of recent years that have been briefly passed in review in the last few pages. Underlying our analysis here and throughout this volume is a theory which, stripped to its barest essentials, sees the mature monopoly capitalist economy as one that is subject to, and indeed dominated by, a basic contradiction: the very growth of its productive potential puts insuperable obstacles in the way of making full use of available human and material resources for the satisfaction of the needs of the great mass of the population. What this means is (1) that in the absence of sufficiently powerful counteracting forces, the normal state of the economy is stagnation; and (2) that the real history of the system in its monopoly capitalist phase is determined by the interaction of the tendency to stagnation and the forces acting counter to this tendency.

On the face of it, this dialectic appears to be quite symmetrical—force versus counterforce, now one and now the other having the upper hand and neither able to establish long-run domination. But this is an illusion. The tendency to stagnation is inherent in the system, deeply rooted and in continuous operation. The counter-tendencies, on the other hand, are varied, intermittent, and (most important) self-limiting. We can best appreciate this lack of symmetry, not by an abstract argument but by a quick review of the history of the last half century. Stagnation reigned supreme in the 1930s, the counteracting forces generated by the First World War and its aftermath having exhausted their strength by 1929. The Second World War put an end to this phase; and the normal aftermath boom took over and played a dominant role for an unusually long period—during which, however, as noted above, the manifestations of the tendency to stagnation never completely disappeared. By the 1970s the forces that powered the long aftermath expansion finally petered out, and stagnation once again rose to dominance. At this juncture, a new set of counteracting forces which have been the focus of our analysis in this introduction went into operation, braking the slide into stagnation and maintaining for a few years a precarious balance between the underlying tendency and the counteracting forces. Once again, however, the latter have shown themselves to be essentially unstable and temporary. As we write these lines, the financial explosion that has speeded up so dramatically in the Reagan period is more and more obviously headed for a crisis.

If this analysis is correct, it has extremely important implications for all those, whether they consider themselves to be on the left or not, who are dissatisfied with the way the economy has been functioning in recent years. The reason is that it rules out the possibility of successful remedial action that leaves intact the system's basic structure and working principles—or, in other words, that does not call into question the primacy of profit-making and capital-accumulation as the purpose and motor force of economic activity. Stagnation theory tells us—and history confirms—that a system so oriented and motivated is not, as mainstream economics has always claimed, a self-adjusting and self-steering organism that automatically adheres to the path of long-run development. On the contrary, it is always tending to bog down under the weight of its own contradictions, and the conditions that foster a new lease on life, like major wars and speculative manias, do enormous damage and soon lose their efficacy.

Stagnation theory, in short, teaches us that what we need is not the reform of monopoly capitalism but its replacement by a system that organizes economic activity not for the greater glory of capital but to meet the needs of people to lead decent, secure, and, to the extent possible, creative lives. Once this lesson has been well and truly learned, we can give up the absurd fantasy of making a rotten system work for us, and buckle down to the increasingly urgent tasks of directly fighting for what ought to be the birthright of every member of a society that has any claim to consider itself free and democratic—a job, a steady income, a home, health care, and security in old age. If our ruling class and the government it controls cannot meet these elementary human demands, they should be thrown out and make way for another system that can and will. It is of course bound to be a long and difficult struggle, but it is the only one that makes sense.

# I

## *Stagnation*

# *Why Stagnation?*

The question "Why Stagnation?" has a rather special significance for me. I started my graduate work in economics exactly 50 years ago this year. The cyclical downturn which began in 1929 was nearing the bottom. Unemployment in that year, according to government figures, was 23.6 percent of the labor force, and it reached its high point in 1933 at 24.9 percent. It remained in the double-digit range throughout the decade. Still, a recovery began in 1933, and it turned out to be the longest on record up to that time. Even at the top in 1937, however, the unemployment rate was still 14.3 percent, and it jumped up by the end of the year. That also happens to be the year I got my Ph. D. Can you imagine a set of circumstances better calculated to impress upon a young economist the idea that the fundamental economic problem was not cyclical ups and downs but secular stagnation?

In the wake of the sharp recession of 1937, a debate over the causes of stagnation began to spread in the economics profession. The two most prominent protagonists were Alvin Hansen and Joseph Schumpeter, Harvard's top economists of the 1930s. Hansen's position was best summed up in his 1938 book *Full Recovery or Stagnation?*, Schumpeter's in the last chapter of his two-volume 1939 treatise on *Business Cycles.*

Schumpeter labeled Hansen's theory the "theory of vanishing investment opportunities," and it is an apt

---

This article is a reconstruction from notes of a talk given by Paul M. Sweezy to the Harvard Economics Club on March 22, 1982. It originally appeared in the June 1982 issue of *Monthly Review.*

characterization. According to this theory, the modern developed capitalist economy has an enormous capacity to save, both because of its corporate structure and because of the very unequal distribution of personal income. But if adequate profitable investment opportunities are lacking, this saving potential translates not into real capital formation and sustained growth but into lowered income, mass unemployment, and chronic depression, a condition summed up in the term stagnation. (The framework of this analysis was of course derived directly from Keynes's *General Theory* which was published in 1936, and of which Hansen was the best known interpreter and champion on this side of the Atlantic.)

To complete the theory, what was needed was an explanation of why there should be such a dearth of investment opportunities in the 1930s as compared to earlier times. Hansen's attempt to fill this gap ran in terms of what he considered to be certain irreversible historical changes which had begun to build up in earlier decades and finally came to dominate the scene after what Schumpeter called the "world crisis" beginning in 1929. To oversimplify somewhat, these changes, according to Hansen, were (1) the end of geographical expansion, sometimes put in terms of the "closing of the frontier" but interpreted by Hansen in a wider global sense; (2) a decline in the rate of population growth; and (3) a tendency on the part of new technologies to be less capital-using than in earlier stages of capitalist development. In Hansen's view, all these changes operated to restrict the demand for new capital investment and in this way transformed the system's great capacity to save into a stagnation-producing force rather than an engine of rapid growth.

Hansen's critics, including Schumpeter, could see little merit in this theory. Not that they denied the necessity for healthy capital formation to sustain growth and high employment: they just couldn't accept the argument that the changes Hansen pointed to were real, or if they were real that they would necessarily entail a weakening of the demand for new investment. The end of geographical expansion in the United States came in the late nineteenth century: Why should it begin to have such adverse economic effects three or four decades later? Population growth doesn't necessarily stimulate investment: it can just as well mean more unemployment, doubling up in housing, a lower standard of living. And the alleged nature and effect of changes in technological innovation were unproved and, according to the critics, unprovable.

Opposed to Hansen's theory, Schumpeter put forward another one which he posed in a somewhat different way. Instead of asking what caused the stagnation of the 1930s, he asked why the cyclical upswing which began in 1933 came to an end so far short of what he and others had always assumed to be the "normal" situation at the end of the prosperity phase of the cycle—full employment, rising prices, tight credit, etc. Some of you will remember that Schumpeter classified economic cycles into three types, each named after an earlier investigator of these phenomena: "Kitchins" (very short, basically inventory cycles); "Juglars" (what most writers think of as *the* business cycle); and "Kondratieffs" (a supposed cycle of some 50 years duration, the reality of which Schumpeter believed in). The experience of the 1930s he described as "the disappointing Juglar." Why?

Rejecting the Hansen theory of vanishing investment opportunities, Schumpeter blamed the anti-business climate of the period—a climate, incidentally, which he thought was an inevitable by-product of capitalist development. In a sense this might be called the "New Deal theory of stagnation," and in one form or another it was shared by most political conservatives. But Schumpeter, as was his wont, gave it a special twist: for him the heart of the matter was not so much the content of New Deal legislation—which he recognized as being compatible with the normal functioning of capitalism—as the personnel who administered the legislation and what he considered the anti-business spirit in which they acted. These, he believed, had a dampening, repressive effect on entrepreneurs' confidence and optimism, blighting their hopes for the future and inhibiting their investment activities in the present.

It was of course no accident that this debate over stagnation flourished in the aftermath of the sharp cyclical decline of 1937-38. Prior to that it seemed reasonable to hope that the long upswing that began in 1933 would continue to capacity production and full employment. The downturn therefore came as a rude shock. With the unemployment rate jumping up to 19 percent in 1938 and remaining over 17 percent in 1939, the grim reality of stagnation could no longer be denied. Hansen's 1938 book and Schumpeter's response of the next year were only the highlights of what gave every sign of becoming one of the classic controversies in the history of economic thought. Nor was it only economists who were involved: Franklin Delano Roosevelt, his once hopeful New Deal blighted by a new and unexpected economic calamity, appointed a high-level Temporary National Economic Committee to find out what went wrong and what could be done about it. But before the TNEC could even begin to report its (ultimately very meager) findings, the Second World War came along. Overnight the whole subject of stagnation dropped out of sight, never to be revived.

After the war, in 1952, one serious and important study of the subject was published in England, *Maturity and Stagnation in American Capitalism*, by Josef Steindl, an Austrian refugee who had spent the war years at the Oxford Institute of Statistics. But it was ignored by the economics profession, and the long period of postwar capitalist expansion which was under way by the time the book appeared seemed to have relegated the whole "problematic" of stagnation to the realm of historical curiosities.

More recent events, however, have shown that the burial of stagnation was, to say the least, premature. I hardly need to remind you that by the mid-1970s the problem was back again, this time with a new twist reflected in a new name, "stagflation." Just when it reappeared could be the subject of debate. Perhaps it was the late 1950s, with the Vietnam war acting as a temporary postponing factor. Perhaps it was the early 1970s, following the Penn-Central credit crunch and Nixon's formal abandonment of the gold standard and brief experiment with wage and price controls. Or perhaps the real return of stagnation should be dated from the recession of 1974–75. In any case the second half of the 1970s displayed the phenomenon in its new form of stagflation for all to see. And there can be little doubt that it has been getting worse since then, as two sets of facts eloquently testify. First, unemployment in the advanced capitalist world (24 OECD countries) is expected to reach 30 million this year, a rate of around 10 percent of the total labor force (with figures much higher of course for women, young people, and minorities). Second, in the United States there have been two recessions in successive years, with the present one quite possibly degenerating into a full-scale depression. (This is not to suggest that those who are expecting or predicting an upturn in the near future are necessarily wrong. There was a brief upturn in 1930 and of course the long recovery already alluded to from 1933 to 1937: indeed ups and downs around the trend, which itself may be up or down, are always not only possible but inevitable.)

I do not pretend to keep up with the latest economic literature as it appears, but it is my impression that the economics profession has not yet begun to resume the debate over stagnation which was so abruptly interrupted by the outbreak of the Second World War. I have the feeling that if you ask an economist how we got into the mess we are in, he or she, while not denying that it is indeed a mess, will reply by giving advice as to how to get out of it but will not have anything very enlightening to say about how we got into it. Leonard Silk, the well-informed, middle-of-the-road economics editor of the *New York Times* is a good example. In many of his columns lately he has been emphasizing the precariousness of the present economic situation, criticizing the policies of the Reagan administration and suggesting ways to do better. In one such column – in the "Business" section of the Sunday paper for March 14th – he even included a considerable amount of background material, centering on five charts dating to 1965, showing that the roots of the problem go back a long way. The headline on the piece is interesting: "What's Happening Is Not a Depression. It's a Chronic State of Unemployment and Industrial Slack. The Government Caused It." At first glance this might seem to be both a description of stagnation and an explanation of it. But if you read the article, you won't find much in the way of explanation. This is hardly surprising since there have been five different administrations since 1965 with a variety of ideologies and policies, and it would seem *a priori* rather unlikely that one would be able to distill out of the whole experience an entity deserving the name "the" government on which to place the blame. Nor does Leonard Silk really try to do so. One rather suspects that some harried editor wrote the headline without reading the article too carefully.

So we still have the question: "Why Stagnation?" It was

raised and then dropped without any satisfactory answer in the 1930s. Reality is now posing it again. I think it is time to accept the challenge and resume the search for an answer.

I think we will do well if we begin where Hansen began in the 1930s. The structure of the economy in both its corporate and its individual dimensions is basically the same as it was a half century ago. Its saving potential is still enormous, and what changes have taken place have tended to make it greater rather than smaller in the intervening period. Corporate concentration has increased, and the distribution of individual incomes remains highly unequal. Moreover, changes in the tax structure have been more and more favorable to the corporations and the rich. As always under such conditions, a strong and sustained investment performance is needed to prevent the economy from falling into stagnation. And that is precisely what has been missing for a long time now, and especially in the last few years. So the immediate cause of stagnation is the same now as it was in the 1930s—a strong propensity to save and a weak propensity to invest.

Let me digress for a moment to point out that the fact that the overall performance of the economy in recent years has not been much worse than it actually has been, or as bad as it was in the 1930s, is largely owing to three causes: (1) the much greater role of government spending and government deficits; (2) the enormous growth of consumer debt, including residential mortgage debt, especially during the 1970s; and (3) the ballooning of the financial sector of the economy which, apart from the growth of debt as such, includes an explosion of all kinds of speculation, old and new, which in turn generates more than a mere trickle-down of purchasing power into the "real" economy, mostly in the form of increased demand for luxury goods. These are important forces counteracting stagnation as long as they last, but there is always the danger that if carried too far they will erupt in an old-fashioned panic of a kind we haven't seen since the 1929–33 period.

So at bottom we are back where the debate of the 1930s left off: Why is the incentive to invest so weak? Hansen's answers are, I think, a good deal less, not more, persuasive today than they were when he first advanced them. And surely no one can follow the Schumpeter line of blaming anti-business policies for discouraging capitalists from investing in the years since the Second World War, least of all with an administration in power like the one we now have in Washington. We must look elsewhere.

I suggest that the answer is to be found in analyzing the long period — 25 years or so — which followed the Second World War, during which we did *not* have a problem of stagnation. In fact during that time the incentive to invest was strong and sustained, and the growth record of the economy was perhaps the best for any comparable period in the history of capitalism. Why?

The reason, I think, is that the war altered the givens of the world economic situation in ways that enormously strengthened the incentive to invest. I list in very summary form the main factors: (1) the need to make good wartime damage; (2) the existence of a vast potential demand for goods and services the production of which had been eliminated or greatly reduced during the war (houses, automobiles, appliances, etc.); a huge pool of purchasing power accumulated during the war by firms and individuals which could be used to transform potential demand into effective demand; (3) the establishment of U.S. global hegemony as a result of the war: the U.S. dollar became the basis of the international monetary system, prewar trade and currency blocs were dismantled, and the conditions for relatively free capital movements were created — all of which served to fuel an enormous expansion of international trade; (4) civilian spinoffs from military technology, especially electronics and jet planes; and (5) the building up by the United States of a huge peacetime armaments industry, spurred on by major regional wars in Korea and Indochina. Very important but often overlooked is the fact that these changes were in due course reflected in a fundamental change in the business climate. The pessimism and caution left over from the 1930s were not dissipated immediately, but when it became clear that the postwar boom had much deeper roots than merely repairing the damages and losses of the war itself, the mood changed into one of long-term optimism. A great investment boom in all the essential industries of a modern capitalist society was triggered: steel, autos, energy, ship-building, heavy chemicals, and many more. Capacity was built up rapidly in all the leading capitalist countries and in a few of the more advanced countries of the Third World like Mexico, Brazil, India, and South Korea.

In tracing the causes of the re-emergence of stagnation in the 1970s, the crucial point to keep in mind is that every one of the forces which powered the long postwar expansion was, and was bound to be, self-limiting. This indeed is part of the very nature of investment: it not only responds to a demand, it also satisfies the demand. Wartime damage was repaired. Demand deferred during the war was satisfied. The process of building up new industries (including a peacetime arms industry) requires a lot more investment than maintaining them. Expanding industrial capacity always ends up by creating *over*capacity.

To put the point differently: a strong incentive to invest produces a burst of investment which in turn undermines the incentive to invest. This is the secret of the long postwar boom and of the return of stagnation in the 1970s. As the boom began to peter out, stagnation was fought off for some years by more and more debt creation, both national and international, more and more frantic speculation, more and more inflation. By now these palliatives have become more harmful than helpful, and to the problem of stagnation has been added that of a rapidly deteriorating financial situation.

Does this mean that I am arguing or implying that stagnation has become a permanent state of affairs? Not at all. Some people—I think it would be fair to include Hansen in this category—thought that the stagnation of the 1930s was here to stay and that it could be overcome only by basic changes in the structure of the advanced capitalist economies. But, as experience demonstrated, they were wrong, and a similar argument today could also prove wrong. I do not myself believe that a new war could have the same consequences as it did last time (or as it did on a lesser scale after the First World War). If a new war were big enough to have a major impact on the economy, it would probably become a nuclear war, after which there might be little left to rebuild. But no one can say for sure that there will never be other new powerful stimuli to investment, such, for example, as were provided by the industrial revolution, the railroad, and the automobile in earlier times. What one can say, I think, is that nothing like that is visible on the horizon now. For those who understand this, the lesson is clear enough: rather than wait around for a miracle (or an irretrievable disaster), it is high time to dedicate our thoughts and energies to replacing the present economic system with one which operates to satisfy human needs and not as a mere by-product of the presence or absence of investment opportunities attractive to a relative handful of socially irresponsible capitalists.

Let me close with a few remarks about the relevance of the foregoing analysis to a subject to which economists have been devoting increasing attention in the last few years, i.e., whether or not the history of capitalism has been characterized by a long cycle of some fifty years' duration (what Schumpeter called the Kondratieff cycle). First, we should be clear that the issue here is not whether capitalist development takes place in an uneven fashion with periods of rapid expansion being succeeded by periods of slow (or even no) expansion and vice versa—what have often been referred to as long waves. The empirical existence of long waves in this sense is undeniable, and the ingenuity of statisticians operating with an almost infinite variety of possible statistical sources can be counted on to make out a case for a time sequence of accelerated and retarded growth rates compatible with the existence of an underlying cyclical mechanism.

But *compatibility* with the existence of a cyclical mechanism is entirely different from *proof* of the existence of such a mechanism. The reason for our acceptance of the idea that relatively short cycles exist (i.e., cycles of less than ten years' duration, Schumpeter's Kitchin and Juglar cycles) is that the mechanisms at work can be elucidated analytically as well as verified empirically. The important point is to be able to demonstrate that the two basic phases of the cycle, expansion and contraction, can each be shown to contain the seeds of its opposite. This principle lies at the core of all modern business-cycle theories. To quote what was long a standard textbook on the subject:

> Business cycles consist of recurring alternations of expansion and contraction in aggregate economic activity. . . . The economy seems to be incapable of remaining on an even keel, and periods of expanding activity always and all too soon give way to declining production and employment. Further, and this is the essence of the problem, each upswing or downswing is self-reinforcing. It feeds on itself and creates further movement in the same direction; once begun, it persists in a given direction until forces accumulate to reverse the direction. (Robert A. Gordon, *Business Fluctuations*, New York, 1952, p. 214)

The key phrase is "until forces accumulate to reverse the direction." This occurs in both the expansion and the contraction phases of the normal business cycle, but the symmetry breaks down when it comes to long waves. As we have already noted in the case of the long expansion following the Second World War, the reversal does indeed take place: it is the nature of an investment boom to exhaust itself. But it is equally clear from the experiences of the 1930s and the 1970s that the stagnation phase of a long wave does not generate any "forces of reversal." If and when such forces do emerge, they originate not in the internal logic of the economy but in the larger historical context within which the economy functions. It was the Second World War that brought the stagnation of the 1930s to an end. We still do not know what will bring the stagnation of the 1970s and 1980s to an end—or what kind of an end it will be.

# *Listen, Keynesians*

There is a remarkable consensus among economists of all ideological and political persuasions—conservative, liberal, and radical—that capitalist economies must grow to be healthy, and that the key to growth lies in the capital accumulation or savings-and-investment process.

Accepting this view, we have long been arguing in effect that capitalism, like living organisms, undergoes a natural aging process from birth through adolescence to maturity. In the early period when society's capital stock—mostly means of production and transportation—is being built up from scratch, the opportunities for capital accumulation appear to be virtually unlimited. The more resources that can be diverted from the production of consumer goods (savings), the more can be devoted to production of means of production (investment). Growth is rapid, interrupted only by financial blockages and demand-and-supply disproportionalities. After these blockages and disproportionalities have been eliminated (a function performed by crises and depressions), accumulation and growth resume what soon comes to be assumed to be their normal course.

So it was during capitalism's youth. This was also of course the period of the rise and refinement of political economy (later called economics) as the science of capitalism's laws and tendencies, a period which can be dated from the time of Adam Smith in the last quarter of the eighteenth century to that of Alfred Marshall, which extended into the third decade of the twentieth century. With negligible exceptions the economists of this period, reflecting the historical reality around them, saw

This article originally appeared in the January 1983 issue of *Monthly Review*.

vigorous growth as the essential characteristic of the system and interruptions of growth as a temporary and self-correcting illness.*

In this vision of capitalism, there was no need for a special theory of the demand side of the investment process. The presence of what was for all practical purposes an unlimited demand for additional means of production could be taken for granted. The determination of the actual rate of accumulation was therefore shifted entirely to the supply side of the equation. Marshall's handling of the problem was fairly typical. In a 20-page chapter entitled "The Growth of Wealth," he devoted less than a page to the demand for capital and most of the rest to the supply of savings. On the former he said in part:

> As civilization has progressed, man has always been developing new wants, and new and more expensive ways of gratifying them. The rate of progress has sometimes been slow, . . . but now we are moving on at a rapid pace that grows quicker every year; and we cannot guess where it will stop. On every side further openings are sure to offer themselves, all of which will tend to change the character of our social and industrial life, and to enable us to turn to account vast stores of capital in providing new gratifications and new ways of economizing effort by expending it in anticipation of distant wants. There seems to be no good reason for believing that we are anywhere near a stationary state in which there will be no new important wants to be satisfied; in which there will be no more room for profitably investing present effort in providing for the future, and in which the accumulation of wealth will cease to have any reward. (Alfred Marshall, *Principles of Economics,* 8th edition, 1920)

The belief in the existence of an unlimited demand for

---

* Some students of the history of economic thought might contend that the preceding summary is contradicted by the forebodings of the classical economists beginning with Ricardo and Malthus, which earned early nineteenth-century political economy its reputation as the "dismal science." This is more apparent than real, however. These thinkers, Ricardo foremost among them, argued on the basis of two presumed natural laws, the law of diminishing returns and the Malthusian law of population, that the accumulation of capital would eventually run out of steam because wages and rent would so far eat into profits as to leave capitalists with neither the wherewithal nor the incentive to continue accumulating. It is important to recognize that there was a very strong political-ideological element in this argument: it was more or less deliberately designed to bolster the case for free trade. The abrogation of the corn laws (agricultural protectionism) would effectively repeal the law of diminishing returns as far as England was concerned and thus liberate the accumulation process from its shackles. This goal was attained in 1846, after which the economists stopped worrying about threats to the future growth of capitalism.

additional capital goods has survived to this day in textbooks, popular economic writings, and most strikingly in the supply-side theory which provides the ideological rationalization for the Reagan administration's economic policies. According to this theory, the malfunctioning of the U.S. economy in recent years stems from too much spending and not enough saving, a combination which is supposed to have produced a low growth rate, with its attendant evils of stagnation, falling profits, rising unemployment, and all the rest.

But at just about the time Alfred Marshall was issuing the eighth and final edition of his famous *Principles,* capitalism was well into a transitional period from adolescence to maturity, climaxed by the post-First World War boom of the 1920s in the United States, by then the world's leading capitalist nation. This boom, like others before it, was fueled by a surge of investment, this time especially in the automobile and related sectors (oil, rubber, glass, highway construction, suburban housing). But the boom also displayed new features reflecting fundamental economic changes. Most important were (1) the burgeoning of consumer credit as a booster to the final demand for the products of these leading industries, and (2) a gradual downdrift of the manufacturing capacity utilization rate after 1925. These were clear signs that despite the injection of strong debt-generated demand for consumer goods, the rate of investment which powered the boom of the 1920s was unsustainable. The crisis of 1929 was a crisis of *overaccumulation.*

Previous capitalist crises had also involved overaccumulation in the sense that investment in the preceding booms had, for largely speculative-financial reasons, outrun demand. But this imbalance between investment and demand in earlier crises turned out to be a temporary phenomenon. After a period of deflation and price readjustments, the investment process resumed its stimulative role: the conventional wisdom which took for granted an unlimited underlying demand for investment was thus empirically supported and became ever more firmly entrenched.

That there was something fundamentally different about the crisis of 1929, that in this case overaccumulation was more than a temporary phenomenon and in fact marked a decisive change in the functioning of the system—this was not apparent to anyone in the early years of the Great Depression. It is hardly an exaggeration to say that the entire economics profession at the time expected growth, rooted in the accumulation process, to resume as it always had in the past.* To be sure it was soon recognized that the downturn precipitated by the crisis was unusually sharp and that the recovery would probably be slow and lengthy. But that had happened before—in the 1870s and 1890s—and it was not hard to find what seemed to be satisfactory explanations in the unique events surrounding the First World War and its aftermath.

What finally drove home the message that things really had changed, that (in our metaphor) capitalism's transition from adolescence to maturity had been completed, was the recession of 1937-38. This event was quite unprecedented. It was not a mere short-term setback but a sudden and steep decline at a time when the upswing from the depression which began in 1933 still had a long way to go to reach what by the standards of past business cycles could be considered full recovery. The unemployment statistics tell the essential story. The peak rate of unemployment was registered in 1933 at 24.9 percent of the labor force. This declined by 1937 to 14.3 percent, and then jumped up again to 19.0 percent in 1938. What these figures describe was at the time something new under the capitalist sun—a steep recession in the midst of a deep depression.

How could this be explained? No one had any doubt about the proximate cause—the breakdown of the capital accumulation process. In the first years of the depression net investment not only disappeared, it was actually replaced by net disinvestment, i.e., the using up of more capital than was produced. And such positive investment as did take place in the recovery beginning in 1933 was mainly to replace what had been lost. When this was accomplished, the steam went out of the process again, precipitating the relapse of 1937-38.

Not surprisingly, a generation of economists brought up on the assumption of an unlimited demand for investment (as ex-

* This comes through very clearly in two detailed studies of the period: William E. Stoneman, *A History of the Economic Analysis of the Great Depression in America* (New York: Garland Publishing, 1979); and Dean L. May, *From New Deal to New Economics: The American Liberal Response to the Recession of 1937* (New York: Garland Publishing, 1981).

emplified in the above-quoted passage from Alfred Marshall's *Principles of Economics*) was at a loss to account for such strange goings-on. Could the trouble be not in the *demand* for real investment but in the *supply* of money capital to finance investment? Hardly. That finance was available was evident from the fact that interest rates had fallen to purely nominal levels (treasury-bill rates were 0.14 percent and the Federal Reserve rediscount rate was 1.50 percent in 1936); and any real pickup in the rate of investment would have boosted corporate profits, thus generating the funds for further investment.

What the recession of 1937-38 revealed was thus the total inability of bourgeois economic theory to cope with the new phenomenon of capitalist maturity. We repeat: underlying this theory insofar as it related to economic growth and the nature of economic fluctuations, was the (usually implicit) assumption of an unlimited demand for investment. Given this assumption, interruptions of growth could be caused only by failure of the institutional (financial, governmental) mechanism of the system to function properly. The very idea that such interruptions might flow from the inherent logic of the system itself rather than from the faulty functioning of its mechanism was ruled out in advance.

The first serious challenge to this deeply ingrained orthodoxy came in the form of Keynes's *General Theory of Employment, Interest, and Money,* published in 1936, i.e., shortly before the recession which began late the following year. Although it has not been widely recognized, it was this feature of the *General Theory* which more than anything else marked it as a turning point in the development of bourgeois economic theory. For the first time the possibility was frankly faced, indeed placed at the very center of the analysis, that breakdowns of the accumulation process, the heart and soul of economic growth, might be built into the system and non-self-correcting. The stage was thus set for a sweeping reconsideration of the whole theory of investment.

What the *General Theory* dealt with as a theoretical problem was posed as an intensely practical problem by the recession of 1937-38. The combination sent shock waves through the economics profession, touching off a debate that could and should have developed into the most searching and significant intellectual confrontation the United States had experienced since the anti-slavery struggle of a century earlier. The debate was initiated by the publication in 1938 of Alvin Hansen's *Full Recovery or Stagnation?*, and the issue was joined the following year in the second volume of Joseph A. Schumpeter's monumental treatise on *Business Cycles.** Hansen and Schumpeter were probably the two most prestigious American economists of the 1930s, and the fact that they took the lead in debating this most crucial of all current economic problems seemed to guarantee that one of those "splendid tournaments" in the history of economic thought of which Marx had written was about to take place.**

But it was not to be. Ominous war clouds gathered over Europe in 1938 (Hitler annexed Austria in March, and the Munich Pact sacrificing Czechoslovakia was signed in September), and the outbreak of hostilities in 1939 completed the shift of attention, in the United States as elsewhere, from depression to war preparation. It soon turned out that the two were alternatives not only as objects of public attention but in practice as well. The unemployment rate which remained over 17 percent in 1939 dropped rapidly thereafter until it reached its wartime low of 1.2 percent in 1944.

Not surprisingly, the debate which had begun so auspiciously in the wake of the recession of 1937-38 receded into the background and died out completely after the war. The all but total lack of attention paid by the economics profession to Josef Steindl's penetrating work *Maturity and Stagnation in American Capitalism* (1952) proved, if indeed proof was needed, that the trauma of the 1930s had been forgotten. It is not true, however, that Keynes was forgotten. What did happen in the new postwar conditions was that the emphases of Keynesian theory, as it had been interpreted by Hansen and his followers in the 1930s, were drastically revised. The problem of the long-run demand for investment, on which Keynes's views were very different from those of Marshall, gave way to concern over fluc-

* See "Why Stagnation?" in this volume, pp. 29-38.

** Preface to the second edition of *Capital*, Vol. 1. Marx was referring specifically to the "quarrel between industrial capital and aristocratic landed property," which elicited the participation of England's outstanding economic thinkers in the decade of the 1820s.

tuations in demand for investment in the course of the business cycle. And Keynes's great achievement was now seen not as a highly original contribution to the understanding of capitalism's basic *modus operandi* but as the invention of a set of clever recipes to counteract the ups and downs of the business cycle. In the depression phase monetary policy should aim to lower interest rates, while fiscal policy should deliberately create government deficits in order to stimulate aggregate demand for goods and services, the market being left to determine which goods and services and in what proportions. In the prosperity phase of the cycle this policy mix should be reversed to forestall "overheating" of the economy (a favorite expression): interest rates should be increased, government spending reduced, and taxes raised, with the resulting budgetary surplus being used to repay the debt incurred to finance the preceding deficit.

This was the gist of what gradually came to be called the "new economics." Joan Robinson and some others among Keynes's followers from an earlier period called it Bastard Keynesianism.

The reason why the emerging debate of the 1930s was interrupted and forgotten while Keynes was being turned into a quite ordinary purveyor of business-cycle remedies is obvious: for some three decades after the beginning of the Second World War capitalism seemed to have recaptured its youth.* Recessions were mild, and after every setback investment bounced back at least as vigorously as during any comparable period in the earlier history of capitalism. The old orthodoxy of the unlimited demand for investment, which had been briefly challenged in the 1930s but never overthrown, simply reasserted itself as an unstated axiom of the new economics. The truth is that, apart from claims to be able to control the business cycle, the new economics is fundamentally no different from the old economics. And when the problems of the 1930s—the breakdown of the accumulation process, the onset of stagnation, the soaring of unemployment—began to reappear in the 1970s, the new economists showed themselves to be as helpless as their pre-Second World War ancestors.

---

* We have discussed the reasons for this many times in The Review of the Month. The most recent, very brief summary appears in "Why Stagnation?" this volume, pp. 29-38.

One consequence of this failure of the new economics was to open the door to the inane dogmas of monetarism and supply-side economics and their misbegotten offspring, Reaganomics. Put into practice—to the extent that a combination of incompatible and contradictory policy prescriptions can be put into practice—this monstrosity has made matters worse and looks like continuing to do so for at least another two years. The other main consequence is that the large body of respectable and respected economists who are too intelligent and/or too honest to buy the rubbish that has to be taken seriously in Washington these days are at a loss to offer meaningful advice to policy-makers or to contribute to the formation of an intelligent public opinion on many of the most important issues of our time.

Just how bad the situation has become is well illustrated by the effort of one of the best of the younger economists to find a way out of the impasse we have been discussing. In a remarkably outspoken article in the *New York Times* Sunday magazine section ("The Great Stagnation," October 17, 1982), Lester Thurow, Harvard-trained professor of economics at MIT, presents a grimly accurate description of the present world-wide capitalist crisis, concluding:

> All of which adds up to this: The world economy is likely to continue sinking into the quicksands. We are likely to have more of the rising unemployment and increasing financial distress we have been experiencing for the last three and a half years. There is simply no indication that the Western nations, individually or jointly, have any program or any approach that is capable of turning the tide.

What follows in the article's last paragraph, however, deserves to be awarded the prize for Anti-Climax of 1982: "From the perspective of this economist. . .the solution lies in old-fashioned Keynesian stimulus. Until we are willing to practice it, America and the world are likely to remain mired in what might be called the Great Stagnation." One rubs one's eyes in wonderment. Talk about practicing stimulus! During the 1970s, the decade in which the Great Stagnation set in, there was not one year in which the federal budget was balanced, and the aggregate deficit in the twelve years 1970-81 was over $400 billion. And the Reagan administration, for all its railing against its big-spending predecessors, has set out on a course of tax cuts for the rich and handouts to the Pentagon which promises to make them look like pikers: latest budget estimates project deficits of well over $200 billion a year for a long time to come. Nor is this the only kind of stimulus that has been practiced in recent years: monetary and related banking policies have been crucial ingredients in the unprecedented explosion of private debt which has characterized the entire post-Second World War period. And yet all these multifaceted forms of stimulation have dismally failed to reinvigorate the accumulation process which Thurow, like all other economists, recognizes to be the key to the health of capitalist economies.

Talk of old-fashioned Keynesian stimulus thus turns out to be as irrelevant as the nonsensical chatter of the monetarists and the supply-siders. But this doesn't mean that Keynes is irrelevant. As we noted above, his *General Theory* of 1936 set the stage for a sweeping reconsideration of the whole theory of investment. Unfortunately, this reconsideration never materialized. The late Michal Kalecki, the Polish economist who has justifiably been credited with "inventing the Keynesian revolution" before Keynes, commented on this subject shortly before his death in the following terms:

> Why cannot a capitalist system, once it has deviated downwards from the path of expanded reproduction [growth], find itself in a position of long-term simple reproduction [no growth]? In fact we are absolutely in the dark concerning what will happen in such a situation so long as we have not solved the problems of the determinants of investment decisions. Marx did not develop such a theory, nor has this been accomplished in modern economics. Some attempts have been made in the development of the theory of cyclical fluctuations. However, the problems of the determination of investment decisions involving. . .the long-run trend are much more difficult than in the case of the "pure business cycle." . . . One thing is clear to me: the long-run growth of the national income involving satisfactory utilization of equipment is far from obvious. (*Social Science Information,* December 1968)

We do not mean to suggest that what is needed is simply a "theory of the determinants of investment decisions": the problem is much broader and includes a crucially important historical dimension which has received some attention in recent years from economists attracted by the hypothesis that capitalist development during the last two hundred years or so has taken place in long cycles. All we are saying is that this is a much neglected and underdeveloped area of economic inquiry which can no longer be neglected by any economist who wants to be taken seriously on the most important problems of our time. As far as bourgeois economics is concerned, Keynes started it, and it would seem appropriate for his followers to take up where he left off.

But there are also other reasons why Keynes is relevant. A large part of the *General Theory* was devoted to showing how and why classical and neoclassical economics alike were wrong in assuming that there are built-in tendencies in capitalist economies to operate at full employment and hence to self-correct any deviations from full employment. But he didn't stop there. He went on to give his views on how the state in capitalist societies could and in his opinion should remedy this lack of an automatic regulatory mechanism. In the postwar period, as noted previously, Keynes's followers, or at any rate those who became the prophets of the new economics, vulgarized these opinions to the point of turning Keynesianism into a cure-all for the capitalist business cycle.

Keynes himself, however, while of course concerned with the business cycle, went much further. Anyone who will take the trouble to read the last chapter of the *General Theory* entitled "Concluding Notes on the Social Philosophy Towards Which the General Theory Might Lead," will recognize a mind that carries on in the tradition of critical bourgeois thinkers of the past—those whom Marx, in the Preface to the second edition of the first volume of *Capital* called "disinterested inquirers" as opposed to "hired prize-fighters." Keynes saw clearly that capitalism contained what in the long run was a potentially fatal flaw, and he wanted to eliminate it, not merely patch it over with a band-aid. And in pursuit of this end he was willing to contemplate reforms as radical as the far-reaching equalization of the distribution of income through the eventual elimination of rentier incomes (i.e., interest and rent), and the "somewhat comprehensive socialization of investment." He recognized that the enlargement of the functions of government which these reforms would entail "would seem to a nineteenth-century publicist or to a contemporary American financier to be a terrific encroachment on individualism," a proposition which, if made today, would have to be rated a terrific understatement.

"Is the fulfillment of these ideas a visionary hope?" Keynes asked in a concluding section. "Have they insufficient roots in the motives which govern the evolution of political society? Are the interests which they will thwart stronger and more obvious than those they will serve?" To which he replied: "I do not attempt an answer in this place. It would need a volume of a different character from this one to indicate even in outline the practical measures in which they might be gradually clothed."

We are not suggesting of course that Keynes had the answers or that he would have come up with them in the sequel to the *General Theory* which never got written. What is important is that if he pursued this line of thought he would have had to confront the basic issue of the power of the ruling class. Whether he would have done so, in view of his ideological attachment to capitalism, is naturally a matter of speculation. Readers of MONTHLY REVIEW know that, in contrast to Keynes, we have an entirely different view of what it will take to liberate the enormous latent power of today's advanced economies from the stranglehold of capitalist control. But unlike the establishment economists of our time, including his latter-day followers, Keynes at least knew that there were real and deadly serious problems to be dealt with, and he was not afraid to tackle them. He was a disinterested inquirer, not a hired prizefighter. Are there any of them left today?

# *Supply-Side Theory and Capital Investment*

In light of the evidence, supply-side theory should by now be dead and buried. According to the supply-siders, all that was needed to turn the economy around quickly was the right kind of tax relief. Their crowning achievement was, as officially titled, The Economic Recovery Tax Act of 1981. This act gave corporations an assortment of tax benefits designed to encourage expansion and improvement of productive capacity. Taxes on the income of wealthy individuals were reduced in order to swell the volume of savings. And, believe it or not, the tax reforms were supposed to get people to work harder and longer hours.* All of this, it was solemnly promised, would provide the wherewithal and the incentives for an immediate burst of new investment, which in turn would set off a new and lasting prosperity. But the real world did not behave the way the supply-siders promised it would. Instead of rising, investment, production, and employment in fact kept on declining throughout 1982.

This article originally appeared in the April 1983 issue of *Monthly Review*.

* The height of absurdity in the defense of the tax program was reached by President Reagan's Council of Economic Advisers, which offered the following among the expected achievements of the new act: "With the Federal Government taking a smaller share of the last dollar of earnings, the return to an individual from an extra hour of work or a more demanding job will increase, strengthening the incentive to work more hours, or accept a more demanding job." (*Economic Report of the President*, February 1982, p. 120.) This nonsense was written at the time when, according to the official figures, ten million people were unemployed, millions of workers were on part time because full-time jobs were not available, and all that business could provide to the employed was an average work week of less than 35 hours.

Yet despite the obvious failure of the experiment, supply-side thinking lives on. It has already become embedded in today's textbooks and is being taught in high schools and colleges as a respectable doctrine. Moreover, essential ingredients of the theory have crept into the discourse and policy recommendations of even liberal Keynesians. Perhaps it should not be surprising that these ideas should have penetrated the ideology of our times so quickly and easily. Establishment economists simply have no theoretical apparatus to explain or anticipate the phenomena of recent years: stagnation, persistent and growing unemployment, financial crises, etc. Unwilling or unable to acknowledge the contradictions of capitalism that produce recurrent crises, they eagerly latch on to timeworn theories dressed up in a new guise, no matter how much these theories have been discredited by history and reason.* The more sophisticated of the academic economists of course reject the simplistic aspect of modern supply-side theory which looks to tax reduction as a cure-all. But many of the leading lights of the profession have jumped on the bandwagon to the extent of advocating less consumption as a supposed necessary prerequisite to an upsurge in investment.

Underlying these prescriptions and promises is the belief that supply creates its own demand. If only capitalists could be stimulated to invest more, there would be clear sailing ahead. Investment, it is assumed, generates enough income (wages, profit, rent) to buy back all that is produced. So if the aim is more jobs and income, all that is needed is additional investment. If disproportions between supply and demand for some types of goods arise from time to time, the competitive process will bring them back into balance. In short, the economy as a whole can pull itself up by its own bootstraps.

There is a plausible ring to this doctrine, and perhaps that is why it gets so wide a response. For it is true that investment by capitalists is the generator of economic growth. But it is equally true that investment tends to produce an overaccumulation of capital, which in turn leads to recurrent crises. Kalecki put it succinctly:

---

* On this, see "Supply-Side Economics," in Harry Magdoff and Paul M. Sweezy, *The Deepening Crisis of U.S. Capitalism* (Monthly Review Press, 1981), chapter 20.

The tragedy of investment is that it causes crisis because it is useful. Doubtless many people will consider this theory paradoxical. But it is not the theory which is paradoxical, but its subject—the capitalist economy. (Michal Kalecki, *Essays in the Theory of Economic Fluctuations*. London: Allen & Unwin, 1939, p. 149)

To appreciate this paradox, it will help to use a simplified example. Let us consider what happens in the manufacturing economy, using the following assumptions: (1) Production generates three types of income—wages, profits, and depreciation reserves. (2) Depreciation reserves are used up each year to replace worn-out machinery. (3) Wages are used to buy consumer goods. (For present purposes we ignore the use of some wages for savings and the recourse to credit for the purchase of consumer goods in excess of wages.) And (4) profits are used for investment that will increase capacity either for production of new products or the expansion of output of old products. (Although in part capitalists use income to buy consumer goods, the overwhelming bulk of profits is destined to purchase capital goods.)

Ideally, under these assumptions, wages will each year equal the output of consumer goods, and profits the output of investment goods. But there is a world of difference between the way these two income streams behave. Once consumer goods are sold, they disappear from the market place and no longer play a role in the economy. (Remember, we are simplifying: there are exceptions, for example the resale of used cars.) Investment goods that are bought with profits are strategically different. They do not disappear from economic activity. Instead, they live on by being added to the stock of already existing and usable capital. As the stock of capital grows, so does productive capacity. At some point in this self-expansion of the capital stock, however, a point is reached where the effective demand for consumer goods is insufficient to warrant further investment.

Since capitalists use their profits in order to make more profits, they will invest only if at the end of the investment process they can sell the final goods. Unable to sell all the goods produced (or, as Marx would put it, to realize all of the surplus value), capitalists slow down or reduce their investment. Profits are hoarded or used for speculation. When this happens, demand is insufficient to buy back the potential output of *both* consumer and producer goods, and the economy turns down. Marx explained it in the following fashion:

> The conditions of direct exploitation and those of the realization of surplus value are not identical. They are separated logically as well as by time and space. The first are only limited by the productive power of society, the last by the proportional relations of the various lines of production and by the consuming power of society. (*Capital,* vol. 3, Kerr edition, p. 286)
>
> But to the extent that the productive power develops, it finds itself at variance with the narrow basis on which the condition of consumption rests. On this self-contradictory basis it is no contradiction at all that there should be an excess of capital simultaneously with an excess of population [i.e., unemployment]. For while a combination of these two would indeed increase the mass of the surplus value, it would at the same time intensify the contradiction between the conditions under which this surplus value is produced and those under which it is realized. (*Ibid.,* p. 287)

The role of investment as the decisive factor in economic crises is most vividly demonstrated by the changes that took place during the Great Depression of the 1930s. As can be seen in Table 1, fixed investment declined over 70 percent as compared with a little over 20 percent in consumption between 1929 and 1933. Consumption held up better because as much

*Table 1*

*Investment vs. Consumption in the Great Depression*

| | *Fixed Investment* | | | *Consumption Expenditures* | | |
|---|---|---|---|---|---|---|
| | *Total* | *Non-residential Structures* | *Producers' Durable Equipment* | *Total* | *Durable Goods* | *Nondurable Goods* |
| | | | *In billions of 1972 dollars* | | | |
| 1929 | 37.5 | 21.1 | 16.4 | 215.1 | 20.9 | 194.2 |
| 1933 | 10.4 | 5.0 | 5.5 | 170.5 | 10.7 | 159.8 |
| 1939 | 20.9 | 8.7 | 12.1 | 219.8 | 18.6 | 201.2 |
| | | | *Index numbers, 1929=100* | | | |
| 1929 | 100.0 | 100.0 | 100.0 | 100.0 | 100.0 | 100.0 |
| 1933 | 27.7 | 23.7 | 33.5 | 79.3 | 51.2 | 82.3 |
| 1939 | 55.7 | 41.2 | 73.8 | 102.2 | 89.0 | 103.6 |

SOURCE: National Income and Product Accounts as reported in various issues of the *Survey of Current Business.*

wages as were earned (plus government relief and past savings) were spent for consumer goods. But in the absence of adequate demand for consumer goods, expanding capacity was out of the question. Hence, there was no demand for machines used to make other machines (e.g., machine tools), or for machines that would add to capacity to produce consumer goods. On the whole, investment was restricted to the barest minimum to maintain factories and equipment needed to meet consumer demand. Since equipment wears out faster than factories, the decline in expenditures for the former was less than for the latter. And since the stock of accumulated capital had a productive capacity far in excess of demand, a considerable portion of capital equipment went into disrepair.

The pattern during the upturn from 1933 to 1939 is noteworthy. On the way up from the 1933 trough, capacity that had long been idle and unattended to had to be put back in working order. Investment therefore forged ahead. But what is significant is that while by 1939 consumption exceeded the 1929 level, investment expenditures were still about 44 percent below the previous high. In the absence of profitable opportunities, and in view of the still large excess of productive capacity, investment acted as a depressant rather than as an engine of growth. This situation did change, but only after the outbreak of the Second World War, when a flood of orders for military goods arrived from Britain and France. Profits in the armaments business were very attractive, and the new type of production called for new equipment. Only then did investment edge up above the 1929 level.

The business cycles since the Second World War have been relatively mild. They did not resemble the Great Depression in either the depth or duration of the decline. Nevertheless, the role of the decline in investment as a major element in contractions shows up in this period as well. Thus, as shown in Table 2 (see p. 55) changes in consumption expenditures during these declines were insignificant, ranging from a 2.3 percent increase to a 2.6 percent decline. But since sales of consumer goods were relatively stagnant and the profit outlook for new investment dim, the expenditures for producers' durable goods (machinery and equipment) fell significantly during each recession. The

*Table 2*
*Consumption During Recessions Since the Second World War*

| *Period of Business Decline** | *Expenditures for Producers' Durable Goods* | *Consumption Expenditures* |
|---|---|---|
| | *Percent Change* | |
| 1948-49 | –22.5 | +2.3 |
| 1953-54 | – 9.6 | +0.7 |
| 1957-58 | –19.3 | –0.1 |
| 1960-61 | –10.8 | 0.0 |
| 1969-70 | – 7.7 | +2.2 |
| 1973-75 | –14.3 | –1.3 |
| 1979-80 | – 7.1 | –2.6 |
| 1981-82** | – 9.5 | +0.7 |

* The percent changes are from peak to trough of producers' durable goods expenditures in each recession. All data used for these calculations are in constant dollars.

** 1982 data are for the third quarter of that year.

SOURCE: Same as Table 1.

differences in the rate of decline between one recession and another are due to a variety of factors, which would require analysis of the concrete conditions of each downturn. The important thing to note for our present purpose is the consistency of the investment declines. Supply did not create its own demand in these recessions largely because the profits of corporations were not used for investment. That was not due to the obstinacy of capitalists or a shortage of money capital, but to the logic of a system operating on the profit motive.

Thus far we have discussed what Kalecki called the "tragedy of investment." But what about the longer-term movements of capital investment as a growth stimulus—its "useful" feature? Indeed, investment did grow throughout the postwar period as a whole. During the recovery phases of each business cycle, investment recovered and then went on to new highs. It did not, however, advance enough to provide employment for all of the growing labor force. Unemployment has been persistently rising ever since the mid-1950s. Moreover the stimulating effect of investment has been petering out. This can be seen from an inspection of Table 3. On the whole, the increases in investment were substantial from the 1958-65 average to that of 1966-73, rising 72.7 percent for producers' durable goods and 40.2 percent in the case of nonresidential structures. Thereafter, the increases get smaller and smaller, with spending on structures actually declining in the last three years.

*Table 3*
*Fixed Investment, 1958-1982*

| | *Producers' Durable Goods* | | *Nonresidential Structures* | |
|---|---|---|---|---|
| | *Annual average** | *Percent change*** | *Annual average** | *Percent change*** |
| 1958-65 | 41.4 | —— | 31.6 | —— |
| 1966-73 | 71.5 | +72.7% | 44.3 | +40.2% |
| 1974-79 | 98.8 | +38.2% | 51.4 | +16.0% |
| 1980-82 | 117.4 | +18.8% | 50.9 | - 1.0% |

* In billions of 1972 dollars.
** Change from preceding period.
Source: Same as Table 1. 1982 data are for the first three quarters.

There is, however, an especially striking aspect to this slowing down in the growth of investment which emerges when we examine what lies behind the averages (see Table 4, p. 8). Looking first at the top part of the table, we find that what has been sustaining investment has been the purchase of communications and high-technology equipment. Thus between 1966-73 and 1974-79, the $12.9 billion annual average increase in investment in communications and high-technology equipment ($27.2–$14.3) accounted for almost half of the $27.3 billion increase in total purchases of producers' durable equipment ($98.8–$71.5). In the last three years, the increase in investment in advanced technology was larger than the total: $20.8 billion ($48.0-$27.2) vs. $18.6 ($117.4–$98.8). What we have here is a much clearer picture of the nature of the investment retardation since 1973. In the case of the more traditional industries, a marked slowing down has taken place as a result of the typical previous overexpansion of capacity relative to demand, as discussed above. And although investment in the newer industries and products has been buoyant, it has not been sufficient to prevent slowing down of investment as a whole.

*Table 4*
*Components of Fixed Investment, 1958-1982*

| | 1958-65 | 1966-73 | 1974-79 | 1980-82 |
|---|---|---|---|---|
| ***Producers' Durable Goods*** | *— Billions of 1972 $s, annual averages —* | | | |
| Communications and high-technology equipment | 6.6 | 14.3 | 27.2 | 48.0 |
| Heavy industrial equipment | 13.1 | 20.9 | 24.3 | 25.4 |
| Transportation equipment | 10.7 | 19.7 | 25.6 | 23.1 |
| Construction and agricultural equipment | 5.0 | 7.6 | 9.9 | 7.4 |
| Other | 6.0 | 9.0 | 11.8 | 13.5 |
| Total | 41.4 | 71.5 | 98.8 | 117.4 |
| ***Nonresidential Structures*** | | | | |
| Commercial | 7.9 | 11.6 | 13.2 | 15.3 |
| Public utilities | 6.9 | 11.5 | 14.8 | 11.8 |
| Oil drilling and mining | 3.5 | 3.1 | 5.4 | 7.6 |
| Industrial | 5.0 | 7.8 | 7.5 | 7.2 |
| Institutional | 6.6 | 7.4 | 6.1 | 5.9 |
| Farm | 1.5 | 1.9 | 3.4 | 2.4 |
| Other | .2 | 1.0 | 1.0 | .7 |
| Total | 31.6 | 44.3 | 51.4 | 50.9 |

SOURCE: Same as Table 1. The classifications of the components follow those of Garri J. Schinasi, "Business Fixed Investment: Recent Developments and Outlook" in *Federal Reserve Bulletin,* January 1983. The 1982 data are for the first three quarters.

Another aspect of the slowdown in business investment is shown in the bottom half of Table 4. The main growth of structures since 1973 has occurred in commercial building (e.g., office buildings, retail stores, fast-food restaurants) and mining and oil drilling, the latter of course in response to the leaps in oil prices at the end of 1973 and 1979. But this expansion was not large enough to prevent a decline in total investment in nonresidential structures. Note especially the reduction in spending for new industrial structures since the 1966-73 period. Clearly, building new factories is not on the order of the day when the problem for business is to sell the output of existing factories.

All in all, the story told in Table 4 is one of creeping stagnation. This, it needs to be stressed, is not due to insufficient profits or a shortage of money. Where vigorous markets exist—as for the products of the new technologies—money is available and investment is flourishing. But strong as these sectors are, their magnitude is not enough to make up for the sluggishness due to excess capacity that has emerged in most manufacturing industries. Nor have the new technologies proven to have the kind of secondary effects that lead to sustained prosperity of the economy as a whole.

The business recovery that may now be underway appears to be a normal inventory correction. During the upward swing of the cycle, production is geared to meeting current demand *plus* replenishing inventories. If a shoe store, for example, experiences a rise in demand, it has to stock up on an assortment of styles and sizes. The same need for inventories holds in general for retailers, wholesalers, and producers of intermediate products. If a seller does not have an adequate reserve on hand to suit customers, potential sales will be lost to better-stocked competitors. A build-up of inventories throughout the economy creates additional jobs and income, helping to pull the economy up. But once the inventory pipelines are filled, and in the absence of other stimuli, production is needed only to meet current consumer demand. At this point production, employment, and wages begin to fall. Eventually production declines below current consumer demand, since part of the demand is met from the oversupply of inventories. Once the excess inventories are sold off, production starts moving up again, if only to meet current demand. The upswing in manufacturing activity can initiate a general upturn: employees are hired, income and consumer demand rise, and the inventory pipelines are refilled again.

This sort of recovery, however, does not assure continued economic growth, nor in today's economy does it create jobs for the mass of the unemployed. In a capitalist economy, jobs on the required scale can be generated only by a vigorous and enduring expansion of business investment. The picture of stagnating investment analyzed above provides little reason for optimism on that score.

# *Unemployment: The Failure of Private Enterprise*

Toward the end of the Second World War, the advancing Allies, with victory in sight, began to plan for a new era of peace and prosperity. Harmonious relations among states, it was held, required not only an international body to resolve disputes but, equally important, a program to overcome the economic strains that contribute to the intensification of rivalries among nations. Thus, the Charter of the United Nations contained the following:

> With a view to the creation of conditions of stability and well-being which are necessary for peaceful and friendly relations among nations based on respect for the principle of equal rights and self-determination of peoples, the United Nations shall promote: (a) higher standards of living, full employment, and conditions of economic and social progress and development. . . . (Article 55)
>
> All members pledge themselves to take joint and separate action in cooperation with the Organization for the achievement of the purposes set forth in Article 55. (Article 56)

Government acknowledgment of responsibility to achieve and maintain full employment was a new departure in the history of capitalism. Earlier conventional wisdom limited the state's obligation with respect to employment to the provision of a suitable environment for the expansion of private industry. The trauma of the Great Depression, the devastation brought about by the Second World War, revolutionary stirrings around the world, and the example set by the Soviet Union that national planning could eliminate unemployment—all this con-

This article originally appeared in the June 1983 issue of *Monthly Review*.

tributed to the novel adoption, in words at least, of full employment as a major aim of government policy.

President Roosevelt went even further in the midst of war. The Bill of Rights, incorporated in the first ten amendments to the Constitution, was, he claimed, "inadequate to assure us equality in the pursuit of happiness." In addition to political rights, economic rights also had to be guaranteed for the sake of "economic security and independence." He therefore called for a second Bill of Rights which would include the right for all, "regardless of station, race or creed," to a decent home, adequate medical care, and protection from the economic fears of old age, sickness, accident, and unemployment. But first and foremost, Roosevelt listed:

> The right to a useful and remunerative job in the industries or shops or farms or mines of the nation.
>
> The right to earn enough to provide adequate food and clothing and recreation *(Message to the Congress on the State of the Union, January 11, 1944).*

In keeping with these aims, Senators Murray and Wagner introduced a Full Employment Bill which declared: "All Americans able to work and seeking work have the right to useful, remunerative, regular, and full-time employment, and it is the policy of the United States to assure the existence at all times of sufficient employment opportunities. . . ."

This statement of purpose, along with the proposed measures to implement a full-employment policy, alarmed the business community, which rallied to defeat the measure. But given the temper of the times and popular support for the Murray-Wagner bill, Congress found it necessary to go ahead with at least a token measure. The result was the Employment Act of 1946, from which all references to a government guarantee of full employment were eliminated. All that finally came out of the political struggle and the fine aims advocated by Roosevelt and the United Nations Charter was the establishment by this Act of a Council of Economic Advisers and the requirement that the president deliver an Annual Economic Report to Congress. Ostensibly, the purpose of the Council and the Annual Economic Report was to supply the information and guidance needed for action that would promote a high level of employment and a minimum of unemployment.

It took some time before it became generally recognized that the Employment Act of 1946 was an empty facade.* The issue of unemployment was for some time swept under the rug, since for a considerable time after the war the number of jobless appeared to be relatively small. During the first eight years following the passage of the Act, from 1947 to 1954, official data showed an annual average of only 2.6 million unemployed (less than 4 percent of the labor force). This was the beginning of the long wave of postwar prosperity, reflecting the stimulus of the Korean War and remilitarization. In addition, the growth of the armed forces after 1950 removed two million from the civilian labor force, men and women who would otherwise have swelled the ranks of the unemployed. And on top of all that, the official statistics underestimated the number of jobless by at least 50 percent, since workers involuntarily on part time and those discouraged from active job-seeking were not counted among the unemployed.

But it became increasingly difficult to cover up and play down the problem, as unemployment kept on increasing from recession to recession and from one period of recovery to the next. Thus, in the last eight years, from 1975 to 1982, the official record showed an average of 7.6 million unemployed. If correction were made for the underestimate in government statistics, the annual average number of jobless would probably be between 11 and 12 million.

Even this adjustment does not give the full picture. The data on unemployment, it should be stressed, are only averages. The total number of people who experience unemployment in a given period is far larger than the average. For example, if worker A is laid off during the first six months of the year and worker B is jobless during the last six months, the record would show an average of one worker unemployed, while in fact two workers experienced joblessness during the year. The differ-

* An attempt was made in the late 1970s to strengthen the Act. The result was the passage of the Full Employment and Balanced Growth Act of 1978. But this too was a watered-down version of the bill proposed by Senators Hubert Humphrey and Augustus Hawkins and has proven to be a total non-starter.

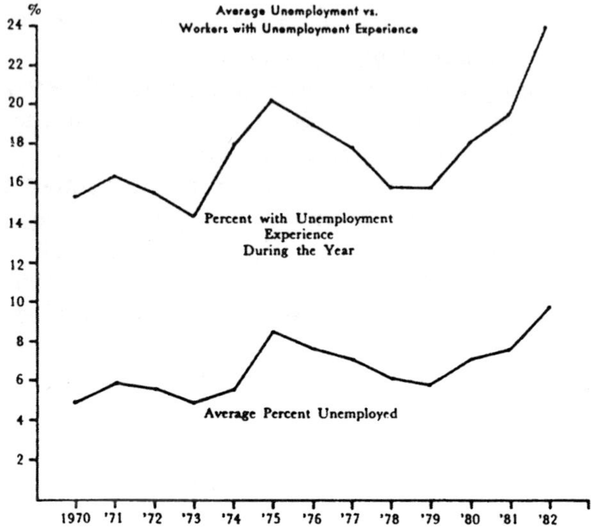


Source: U.S. Labor Dept., *Labor Force Statistics Derived from Current Population Survey: A Data Book*, vol. 1 (BLS Bulletin 2096, Sept. 1982). *Employment and Earnings*, March 1983. The 1982 figure for percent with unemployment experience was estimated based on past relationship.

ence between the two measures—the average versus the total—is portrayed in the accompanying chart. The bottom line shows the average percent unemployed, computed by dividing the average number of unemployed by the average size of the labor force. This is the way unemployment percentages are reported monthly in the press, based on Bureau of Labor Statistics releases. On the other hand, the percent of the labor force that experienced unemployment during the year—shown by the top line of the chart, is about two-and-a-half times the average. Thus, in 1982 average unemployment, according to official data, was 9.7 percent. But in fact about 24 percent of the labor force experienced one or more bouts of unemployment during that year.

Still another aspect of the severity of unemployment needs to be noted. Not only has the number of people out of work reached unconscionable levels, but the duration of unemployment has also reached new highs. At the bottom of the previous recession in 1975, the average duration of unemployment was 15 weeks. In February 1983, the latest month for which such information is available, the average was 19.4 weeks. If we multiply the average number of unemployed by the average number of weeks unemployed, we get a measure of the total weeks of unemployment—a more meaningful indicator of the impact of unemployment. By that measure, the total number of jobless weeks experienced by those unemployed in February 1983 was *twice* that of the last quarter of 1975, the low point of the recession of the mid-1970s.

Now let us see how this social disaster is dealt with by the President's Council of Economic Advisers—the organization that is supposed to guide the country to maximum employment and minimum unemployment. The latest Annual Report of the Council does in fact dwell at length on this issue (*Economic Report of the President,* February 1983, pp. 29-50), but it does so in what is, to say the least, a disingenuous way. At first, it announces solemnly that "unemployment is the most serious economic problem now facing the United States." But then it goes on to explain that at best unemployment cannot be safely reduced below somewhere between 6 and 7 percent. That, it says, is a necessary threshold of unemployment, in order to keep inflation at bay. Moreover, the threshold has been rising. Why? Where does this threshold come from? The Annual Report gives four reasons, which are worth examining.

(1) *The Effect of Demographic Factors.* "Persons with little labor market experience tend to have high rates of unemployment as they move from job to job in order to obtain a desirable career position." (p. 38) The reference here is to the growing number of youths and women entering the labor force. But the facts given in the statistical appendix to the Annual Report prove this argument to be arrant nonsense. Take first the notion that an increasing number of inexperienced women workers cause the threshold of unemployment to rise. It happens that the Bureau of Labor Statistics calculates a separate unemployment rate for "experienced wage and salary workers." If it were true that women entrants to the labor market flit from job to job, one would expect that the unemployment rates of women workers would be higher than those of experienced wage earners. The facts don't show that at all. The average rate of unemployment from 1970 to 1982 among women over 20 years old

was 6.3 percent, precisely the same as that shown for the experienced category.

As for young people, the Council can point to a long-time trend of high unemployment in this category. From this it reaches the conclusion that the more young people enter the labor market, *the higher unemployment has to be*. But the reality is quite the opposite: the fewer the jobs that are available, the more unemployment there will be among the new entrants. The problem is not that there are more "restless" young people moving from job to job, but that the number of jobs available to youths in this age group has been drying up. The rate of unemployment among 16- to 19-year-olds was 9 percent in 1947 and is now almost 25 percent. Over 45 percent of black teenagers in the labor force are currently unemployed. This is hardly the picture of young workers moving from job to job in search of a suitable career. Rather, it is clear-cut evidence of the lack of job opportunities.

(2) *Social Insurance Programs*. "Behavioral effects of social insurance programs such as unemployment insurance include the encouragement of firms to lay off workers and the inducement of persons to prolong their spells of unemployment." (p. 38) Well, well. So employers are philanthropists who would keep unneeded workers on the payroll if they had no other source of income. But because workers can receive unemployment insurance benefits bosses are "encouraged to lay off workers." It would follow that once insurance benefits are exhausted, the unemployed ought to be rehired. This should be welcome news to unemployed auto and steel workers!

The claim that workers voluntarily remain jobless because they receive benefits is as old as the existence of unemployment insurance, and was even heard in the days of the Poor Laws. It is in fact the reactionary's stock in trade. Only those who do not know what it means to pay for a family's food, clothing, housing, and medical expenses on meager and exhaustible insurance benefits can utter such claptrap. And even if there are some among the many millions of unemployed who prefer insurance payments to a regular job, what does that have to do with justifying a supposedly necessary base level of unemployment of 6 to 7 percent? Unemployment insurance was also in effect from 1950 to 1953 when the average rate of unemployment was 3.1 percent!

(3) *Wage Rigidity.* "Increased wage rigidity is likely to raise the economy's inflation threshold level of unemployment, since less flexible wages increase the inevitable unemployment associated with the sectoral shocks which buffet the economy. The reasons for this change are not well understood. A side effect of the provision of a 'safety net' program is that employees may become more resistant to wage reductions, leading to increases in wage and price rigidity." (p. 39) This is pure gobbledygook designed to justify cuts in wages and social welfare. If only workers would work for less pay, there would be more jobs. The fallacy of this hoary doctrine was clearly disproved during the Great Depression. A decline in wage rates would of course contribute to deflation, but it would also contract demand and thus lead to reduced output and even more unemployment.

(4) *Increasing Structural Change.* "Because transfers of human and physical resources are costly and take time, increased unemployment is a concomitant of structural change." Structural change is always present in a dynamic capitalist economy. Rising and declining industries, technological innovations, and regional shifts are constant elements of an expanding capitalism. There is no reason to believe, however, that structural changes in recent years have been greater than in the past. If anything, a case can be made that there have been fewer structural changes in the past decade as a result of the spread of stagnation.

In short, double-talk and reactionary cant is the best the Council of Economic Advisers can offer to explain the present especially high unemployment levels and to justify in advance future excessive joblessness. What the Council and other bourgeois ideologists cannot face up to is that the capitalist system is sick and that the persistence of mass unemployment is a chief symptom of this sickness. Put simply, private enterprise has not been able to provide enough jobs to keep pace with the growth in the population and government has been unwilling to do so. As a result the volume of unemployment has been creeping up since the end of the Second World War, becoming especially severe during downturns of the business cycle. This was so even during the long postwar wave of prosperity. And with the onset of stagnation, a higher and higher level of unemployment has become a permanent feature during the recovery phases of the cycle as well. It is recognition of these facts that has led many economists and business leaders to accept a 6 to 7 percent unemployment rate as "normal."

The weakness of the system as a job provider can be seen in the accompanying table, which presents a breakdown in the growth of jobs between 1970 and 1980. During that period the official unemployment rate grew from 4.8 to 7 percent—a measure of the combined failure of the private economy and all

*Table 1*

*Employment of Wage and Salary Workers*

*(in millions)*

| | | | Increase | |
|---|---|---|---|---|
| | *1970* | *1980* | *Absolute* | *Percentage* |
| Goods Production[1] | 31.6 | 34.1 | 2.5 | 7.9 |
| Wholesale and Retail Trade | 12.5 | 15.7 | 3.2 | 25.6 |
| Eating and Drinking Places | 2.6 | 4.6 | 2.0 | 76.9 |
| Finance, Insurance, and Real Estate | 3.6 | 5.2 | 1.6 | 44.4 |
| Business, Legal, and Accounting Services | 2.1 | 3.9 | 1.8 | 85.7 |
| Health Services | 3.1 | 5.3 | 2.2 | 71.0 |
| All Other Services | 6.3 | 8.7 | 2.4 | 38.1 |
| Government | 12.6 | 16.2 | 3.6 | 28.6 |
| Total | 74.4 | 93.7 | 19.3 | 25.9 |
| Total Labor Force[2] | 82.8 | 106.9 | 24.9 | 29.1 |

[1] Includes agriculture, mining, construction, manufacturing, transportation, and public utilities. The data for agriculture include self-employed as well as wage and salary workers.

[2] Includes the self-employed as well as wage and salary workers and the unemployed.

Note: Totals may not be equal to the addition because of rounding off.

Source: U.S. Department of Labor, *Employment and Earnings, United States, 1909-78*. U.S. Department of Labor, *Supplement to Employment and Earnings, June 1982*. *Employment and Earnings,* March 1983. *Economic Report of the President,* March 1983.

levels of government to provide sufficient remunerative work for the growing labor force, not to mention making up for the previous slack.

What is most striking in this table is the performance of the goods-producing industries: agriculture, mining, manufacturing, construction, transportation, and public utilities. These industries supply whatever dynamism there is in the capitalist system, and as a group provide the largest concentration of jobs. Yet employment in this sector increased by less than 8 percent in this period. The performance of the manufacturing industries (not shown separately in the table) was saddest of all. There were 14.2 million production workers employed in manufacturing in 1980 and 14.0 million in 1970, an increase of only 1.4 percent in 10 years.

In contrast, there was a larger increase in jobs devoted to selling the goods produced. Employment in wholesale and retail trade grew by 3.2 million, as compared with 2.5 million in *all* of goods production. Still more striking was the 3.4 million expansion in employment in financial and business services: 1.6 million in finance, insurance, and real estate; and 1.8 million in business, legal, and accounting services. Thus more and more jobs are concerned with the pecuniary aspects of capitalism (sales, finance, speculation) and less and less with the industrial base.

The largest growth in the number of jobs took place in government (3.6 million). In addition, a considerable portion of the 2.4 million job growth in "all other services" was created by nonprofit organizations (colleges, membership organizations, philanthropic activities), while most of the 2.2 million additional jobs in health services were supported by government financing through Medicare and Medicaid. This is not to imply that the expansion of these areas was not desirable. But it is important to recognize that a large part of the employment growth has been coming from public and not private enterprise.

What this analysis shows is that private enterprise is *increasingly* unable to provide what Franklin Roosevelt four decades ago proclaimed to be the fundamental right of everyone, the right to a "useful and remunerative" job. It is time to draw the appropriate conclusions.

# *The Strange Recovery of 1983-1984*

Even the most sanguine of spokespeople for the business community has long been aware that the problems of the U.S. economy are more serious than the matter of recurrent recessions. Along with worries about interest rates, the international value of the dollar, the trade balance, the federal deficit, the danger of a new flareup of inflation, and the persistence of mass unemployment, there is a general awareness that what matters most is weak economic growth, for which the appropriate remedy is the revitalization of capital investment. Hence the efforts of one Washington administration after another to stimulate investment by means of a whole series of tax concessions to business (see Craig Medlen, "Corporate Taxes and the Federal Deficit," *MR, November* 1984). Yet capital investment has continued to lag.

When the Reagan administration won office, it claimed to have the real answer: drastically reduce the tax burden on the wealthy and on corporations. The sizable tax cuts introduced during Reagan's first term were heralded as opening the floodgates to a new wave of capital investment that would at last generate rapid and sustained economic growth.

What came instead was a severe economic downturn in 1980-82. Not to worry, argued the supply-side advocates, have patience, just give the tax cuts time to take effect. And, as occurs in every business cycle, a recovery did indeed ensue, along with a significant revival of capital investment. This was taken as proof positive of the validity of Reaganomics, a signal of the birth of a new era of prosperity.

But what does this upturn consist of and what does it tell

This article originally appeared in the October 1985 issue of *Monthly Review*.

*Chart 1*
*Nonresidential Fixed Investment*
*(in billions of 1972 dollars)*

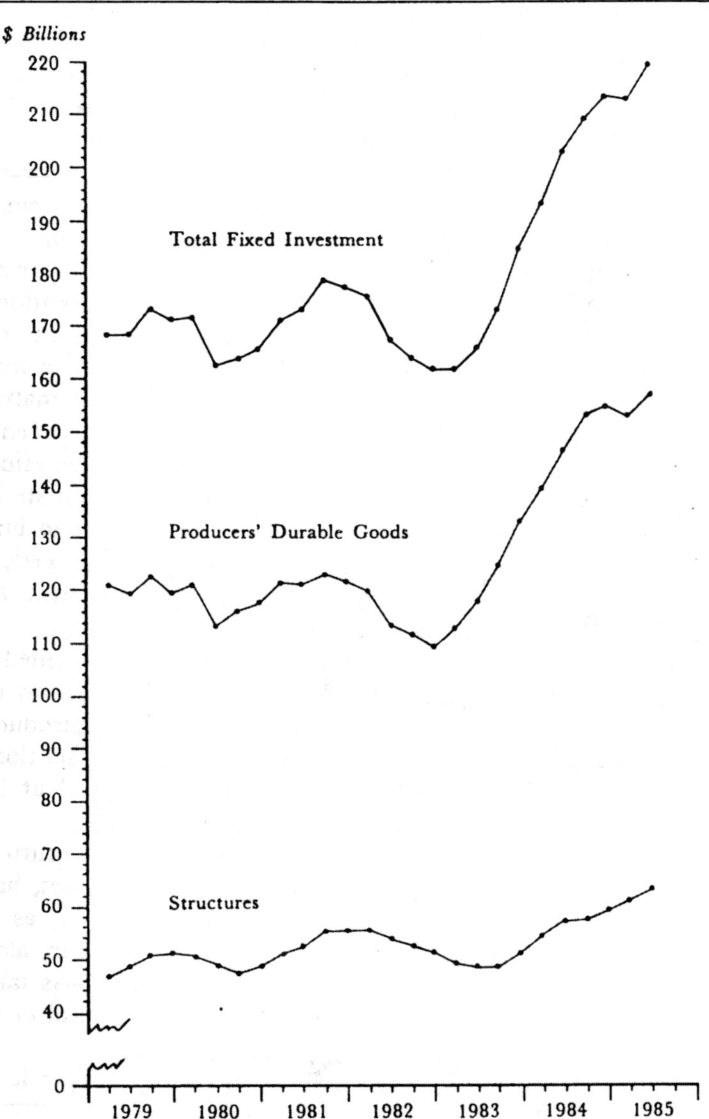


*Source:* National product and income accounts as represented in *Survey of Current Business*, July 1983, July 1984 and July 1985

us about the prospects for the future? To answer these questions, let us first look at the overall picture of fixed business investment as portrayed in the accompanying chart. The top line traces the quarterly fluctuations of total fixed investment beginning with the 1979 peak. The course of the recession can be seen in the dip in 1980, followed by a short recovery to a new peak that lasted only half a year, followed by a sharp second decline in 1982. The real upswing began in 1983, and since then the advance in capital investment has every appearance of vigorous growth, reaching a new high in the second half of 1985, about 30 percent above that of 1979. The two major components of fixed investment, also shown on the chart, exhibit a similar pattern, except that the line tracing investment in producers' durable goods displays more pronounced fluctuations than that tracing investment in structures.

On closer examination, however, this overall picture—the basis for optimistic hopes for the future—turns out to be grossly misleading. When we speak of capital investment, we generally think of factories being built and equipped to churn out steel, cars, chemicals, clothing, processed foods, etc. But in fact spending for manufacturing capacity represents barely 10 percent of what economists include under the rubric of capital investment. According to the accepted way of reckoning, capital investment includes every purchase of a durable good or building used for any business purpose. Thus, the car purchased by a traveling salesman is counted as capital investment, and so is the computer bought by an insurance agent to help stimulate sales. To come to grips with what the big advance in capital spending is all about, we have to look beneath the surface and examine what the summary data consist of. And when this is done a wholly different story emerges: rather than foreshadowing a new wave of growth, the investment pattern of the latest upswing reveals features typical of a period of stagnation.

Tables 1 and 2 tell us what underlies the largest component of fixed business investment, the purchase of durable producers' goods depicted in the middle line of the chart. As of this writing, complete data on the constituent parts of this category are available only through 1984, but what they demonstrate is significant enough. Moreover, the partial data on hand for the first

*Table 1*
*Investment in Producers' Durable Goods*
*(in billions of 1972 dollars)*

| | 1979 | 1980 | 1981 | 1982 | 1983 | 1984 |
|---|---|---|---|---|---|---|
| *Rising sectors* | *49.2* | *52.9* | *60.1* | *61.8* | *69.9* | *85.6* |
| High-tech products[1] | 39.1 | 44.9 | 50.6 | 52.5 | 57.5 | 68.7 |
| Autos for business | 10.1 | 8.0 | 9.5 | 9.3 | 12.4 | 16.9 |
| *Relatively stable sectors* | *19.0* | *19.1* | *19.6* | *17.9* | *18.5* | *21.2* |
| Electrical apparatus[2] | 6.6 | 6.6 | 6.6 | 6.0 | 6.6 | 7.6 |
| Miscellaneous products | 12.4 | 12.5 | 13.0 | 11.9 | 11.9 | 13.6 |
| *Declining sectors* | *53.4* | *45.8* | *43.0* | *33.4* | *33.8* | *41.7* |
| Manufacturing machinery and equipment[4] | 22.0 | 21.4 | 21.0 | 16.8 | 16.2 | 19.3 |
| Transportation other than autos[5] | 20.6 | 15.9 | 14.2 | 11.7 | 12.4 | 16.7 |
| Agricultural and construction machinery | 10.8 | 8.5 | 7.8 | 4.9 | 5.2 | 5.7 |
| *Total*[6] | *121.6* | *117.8* | *122.7* | *113.1* | *122.2* | *148.5* |

*Notes*

1. Computing, accounting, and office machines; communication equipment; instruments.
2. Electrical transmission, distribution, and industrial apparatus; electrical equipment not included in other categories.
3. Furniture and fixtures; service industry machinery; mining and oilfield machinery; etc.
4. Metalworking machines; engines and turbines; general industrial equipment; and fabricated metal products.
5. Trucks, buses, and truck trailers; aircraft; ships; railroad equipment.
6. These totals differ slightly from those given in the national product accounts because minor adjustments are made in these accounts that are not relevant here.

*Source:* National product and income accounts as reported in *Survey of Current Business*, July 1983 and July 1985.

half of 1985 show a continuation of the same tendencies. The two tables deal with the same set of statistics. Table 1 presents the dollar amounts, while Table 2 translates the absolute numbers into indexes which make it easier to get a clear comparison of relative changes since 1979.

What stands out when the durable producers' goods category is analyzed is the existence of three distinctly different sectors. Purchases of some types of investment goods have remained

*Table 2*
*Investment in Producers' Durable Goods*
*(Index numbers: 1979 = 100)*

| | *1979* | *1980* | *1981* | *1982* | *1983* | *1984* |
|---|---|---|---|---|---|---|
| *Rising sectors* | *100* | *107.5* | *122.2* | *125.6* | *142.1* | *174.0* |
| High-tech products[1] | 100 | 114.8 | 129.4 | 134.3 | 147.1 | 175.7 |
| Autos for business | 100 | 79.2 | 94.1 | 92.1 | 122.8 | 167.3 |
| *Relatively stable sectors* | *100* | *100.5* | *103.2* | *94.2* | *97.4* | *111.6* |
| Electrical apparatus[2] | 100 | 100.0 | 100.0 | 90.9 | 100.0 | 115.2 |
| *Declining sectors* | *100* | *85.8* | *80.5* | *62.5* | *63.3* | *78.1* |
| Manufacturing machinery and equipment[4] | 100 | 97.3 | 95.5 | 76.4 | 73.6 | 87.7 |
| Transportation other than autos[5] | 100 | 77.2 | 68.9 | 56.8 | 60.2 | 81.1 |
| Agricultural and construction machinery | 100 | 78.7 | 72.2 | 45.4 | 48.1 | 52.8 |
| *Total*[6] | *100* | *96.9* | *100.9* | *93.0* | *100.5* | *122.1* |

*Notes and source:* same as Table 1.

relatively stable, fluctuating mildly throughout the period. These account for about 15 percent of all investment in equipment. For the rest, we see markedly contrasting trends—on the one hand, a sector that advances rapidly and persistently, and on the other hand, a sector that declines sharply during the recession and, after two years of recovery, still lags behind the preceding 1979 peak.

The point that needs to be specially emphasized is that the overall advance in investment in durable producers' goods is accounted for by two types of goods alone: high-tech products and autos. As can be seen in Table 1, the category as whole took a great leap forward in 1984, surpassing 1979 by almost $27 billion ($148.5–$21.6). At the same time the combined "rising sectors" grew even more—over $36 billion ($85.6–$49.2). In other words, the latter not only made up for the roughly $12 billion drop in the declining sectors, but were the *sole* reason for the much-touted strength of investment in equipment and machinery during the current recovery.

The meaning of this development needs to be fully under-

*Table 3*
*Investment in Structures*
*(in billions of 1972 dollars)*

| | *1979* | *1980* | *1981* | *1982* | *1983* | *1984* |
|---|---|---|---|---|---|---|
| *Rising sectors* | *19.8* | *21.2* | *23.0* | *24.1* | *23.9* | *30.0* |
| Commercial | 13.4 | 14.4 | 15.6 | 16.5 | 15.5 | 20.5 |
| Educational, religious, hospital | 3.1 | 3.3 | 3.5 | 3.9 | 4.2 | 4.2 |
| Hotels, motels, etc.[1] | 3.3 | 3.5 | 3.9 | 3.7 | 4.2 | 5.3 |
| *Relatively stable sectors* | *18.2* | *18.5* | *19.6* | *19.4* | *18.2* | *19.5* |
| Public utilities | 13.5 | 12.6 | 12.0 | 12.0 | 11.8 | 13.0 |
| Oil and natural gas | 4.7 | 5.9 | 7.6 | 7.4 | 6.4 | 6.5 |
| *Declining sectors* | *11.0* | *9.1* | *9.9* | *9.8* | *7.1* | *7.2* |
| Industrial | 8.0 | 6.6 | 7.7 | 7.6 | 5.5 | 5.9 |
| Farm | 3.0 | 2.5 | 2.2 | 2.2 | 1.6 | 1.3 |
| *Total* | *49.0* | *48.8* | *52.5* | *53.3* | *49.2* | *56.7* |

*Note*

1. This is a miscellaneous category that is dominated by the construction of hotels and motels, but also includes buildings for recreational and social activities, passenger terminals, greenhouses, animal hospitals, mining, etc.

*Source:* same as Table 1.

stood if we are to appreciate the nature of the present recovery. The truth is that the two rising sectors are for the most part concerned with making money rather than with making goods—or, as Veblen put it, with pecuniary rather than industrial pursuits. This is not to deny that an important portion of high-tech products are bought by industrial firms. But the uses to which they are devoted have less to do with production than with finance. Computers, communication equipment, etc., are needed to aid in marketing, coordinating farflung multinational empires, reducing the number of jobs on the factory floor, and obtaining greater control over the workforce. Even more important, however, is the enormous demand for high-tech products in the areas of commerce and services. You can see it every time you cash a check at your bank, shop at your supermarket, or buy an airplane ticket at your local travel agent. Without a doubt,

*Table 4*
*Investment in Structures*
*(Index numbers: 1979 = 100)*

| Purpose | 1979 | 1980 | 1981 | 1982 | 1983 | 1984 |
|---|---|---|---|---|---|---|
| *Rising sectors* | *100* | *106.6* | *116.2* | *121.7* | *120.7* | *151.5* |
| Commercial | 100 | 107.5 | 116.4 | 123.1 | 115.7 | 153.0 |
| Education, religious, hospital | 100 | 106.5 | 112.9 | 125.8 | 135.5 | 135.5 |
| Hotels, motels, etc.[1] | 100 | 106.1 | 118.2 | 112.1 | 127.3 | 160.6 |
| *Relatively stable sectors* | *100* | *101.6* | *107.7* | *106.6* | *100.0* | *107.1* |
| Public utilities | 100 | 93.3 | 88.9 | 88.9 | 87.4 | 96.3 |
| Oil and natural gas | 100 | 125.5 | 161.7 | 157.4 | 136.2 | 138.3 |
| *Declining sectors* | *100* | *82.7* | *90.0* | *89.0* | *64.5* | *65.5* |
| Industrial | 100 | 82.5 | 96.3 | 95.0 | 68.8 | 73.8 |
| Farm | 100 | 83.3 | 73.3 | 73.3 | 53.3 | 43.3 |
| *Total* | *100* | *99.6* | *107.1* | *108.8* | *100.4* | *115.7* |

*Note and source:* same as Table 3.

though, the major prop to the headlong upsurge in the use of business computers has come with the explosion in finance. By now practically every broker and trader in stocks, bonds, commodities, interest-rate futures, and foreign exchange is directly tied into an electronic network, a good deal of it international as well as nationwide—all of this to sustain and foster speculative fevers in the process of servicing customers, designing strategies for investment and speculation, and inventing new instruments for speculation. With the aid of the new technologies, bank transactions within the United States and between continents are executed almost instantaneously, and automated deposit-and-withdrawal machines dot the land. The heating up of financial activity in other areas—insurance, real estate, and nonbank finance companies—contributes as well to the burgeoning sales of high-tech products.

The other rising sector, alongside high-tech, is equally distant from industrial pursuits. The fact that business purchases of autos in 1984 were 67 percent above 1979 (see Table 2) is for the most part due to the expansion of car-rental firms, taxicab fleets, and the needs of sales promotion. Some of the unusual jump in 1984 may have been due to the bunching of demand resulting from the recession-induced postponement of car replacements; but whether for replacement or expansion—and taking into account that some of the cars are used to facilitate production or supply transportation services—at bottom the primary business demand for cars has to do with selling rather than production.

In light of the vigorous growth in demand for the products of the rising sectors one might expect a responsive expansion of manufacturing capacity to produce these goods. And that of course has happened in a select number of firms. In addition, the growth in the production of "defense" equipment—50 per--cent between 1979 and 1984, according to the Federal Reserve Board—has no doubt called for a considerable amount of new investment. Alongside all this, moreover, has been the continuing need to replace worn-out and obsolescent machinery. Yet despite such sources of support, the decline in investment in manufacturing as a whole took a deprssion-like 25 percent nosedive during the last recession and was still some 12 percent below the past peak during the second year of recovery (see Table 2).

Clearly, the investment needed to meet the energetic demand in the rising sectors (including armaments) have been far from adequate to invigorate the accumulation of capital in manufacturing industry as a whole. The popular explanation for this weakeness of manufacturing puts the blame on competition from abroad. This is of course a contributing factor, though not as important as is generally believed. The real reason, as we have pointed out many times in this space, is the onset of stagnation, which in turn is associated with an overaccumulation of money capital coupled with lagging growth of consumer demand. The point is that a healthy underpinning of demand for both capital and consumer goods could support growth of both imports and domestic production. Furthermore, the insufficiency of demand shows up in the basic industries where imports do not compete with domestic production. One of these—equipment for electric power production and distribution—did show some strength in 1984. But look at what has been happening to the purchase of transportation equipment other than autos, and agricultural and construction machinery.

As can be seen in Table 2, the former was 19 percent below and the latter 47 percent below the preceding 1979 peak.

Some of the technological revolutions of the past have served to lift capitalist economies out of a stage of stagnation and to set in motion a long period of rapid growth. But those were invariably innovations that had strong secondary effects radiating throughout the basic industries, generally associated with major shifts in population, extensive construction activity, and expansion of auxiliary manufacturing industries. What we have seen thus far in the case of the new electronic and communication technologies is that, apart from their role in the explosion of finance, they have had minor secondary effects in the areas of manufacturing and construction. Despite a good deal of wishful thinking and propaganda, there is thus far no hard evidence or strong logical reasoning on which to base more optimistic expectations for the future.

The divergent trends typical of a period of stagnation—expansion of the pecuniary and contraction of the industrial pursuits—show up equally in the rest of capital investment. Tables 3 and 4 present the data for the constituent parts of investment in structures, the bottom line of the chart. Here too the overall picture reflects recovery and the rise to a new high in 1984. And again it is the rising sectors that account for the recovery. Note that in 1984 commercial structures (e.g., office buildings, shopping centers) were $10 billion ahead of 1979, whereas all of construction for business purposes advanced only $7.7 billion. The two "relatively stable sectors" display minor differences. Construction of public utility structures fluctuates hardly at all throughout the period. Activity in the oil and natural gas field, on the other hand, may at first sight seem like random up-and-down movements. Actually, the key factor here is fluctuations in the price of the final products. The marked rise in activity from 1979 to 1981/82 was in response to the dreams of huge profits to be made when the price of these natural resources rose to unprecedented heights. The subsequent price drop put a damper on new exploration and development, although there was sufficient completion work to be done on previous project starts to keep the level of construction above that of 1979.

From the standpoint of the nature of the recovery, the most significant development is the low performance of industrial and agricultural construction in 1984. The effect of business declines does not show up immediately in recession years because undertakings started during the preceding upswing often take several years to complete. The impact of recession may thus first come to light during the recovery provided that at the same time there is little new activity spurred by the recovery. The lack of a significant rise in construction activity during the current recovery is clearly apparent in the fact, shown in Table 4, that industrial construction in 1984 was 26 percent below that of 1979. The collapse of building on farms—in 1984 almost 57 percent below 1979—is but another sign of the growing crisis in agriculture.

To sum up, the evidence presented here demonstrates that except for selected areas associated with money-making the current recovery is inherently sluggish and reflects a continuation of the stagnation which set in more than a decade ago. We would argue further that this is not an accidental phenomenon but one that is deeply rooted in the nature of a mature capitalist economy. This being the case, the various programs that attack one or another symptom of stagnation stem from illusions about what can be accomplished by mere superficial reforms.

The irony of the miserable performance of capital investment activity is that it shows not only what is wrong but also how much better things could be. For it reveals that the capacity to meet the needs of the people exists, either in the form of idle plant and equipment or the capability to create additional capacity. The clearest case is food. The latest report of the Physician's Task Force on Hunger shows that, apart from widespread malnutrition, at least 20 million people in the United States suffer from hunger at some point during the year. Yet ample supplies are at hand to eliminate hunger and malnutrition, and farmers could easily produce still more surplus food. Furthermore, supplies, machinery, and skilled labor are clearly available to create decent living quarters for the millions of people suffering in inadequate housing. And if it should turn out that existing idle resources were insufficient, a vast amount of resources could be released by cutting down on the wasteful investment in office buildings, as well as by making use of existing idle capacity to produce construction machinery. As can be seen in Table 2, the production of agricultural and construction machinery in 1984 was little more than half that of 1979. And the same goes for the capacity to produce machinery and equipment to be used in the manufacture of goods to satisfy the needs of the people. All that stands in the way is the domination of the profit motive and the market. A recent editorial in *Business Week* (19 August 1985), commenting on a story in that issue on Exxon Corporation's choking on a surplus of cash, stated: "True, the sight of so many companies sitting around on bags of cash they cannot find profitable use for raises some distressing questions about the vitality of the U.S. economy."

Indeed it does.

Of course, removing the constraints of the profit motive and the market is easier said than done. But the more recognition of this reality sinks into the consciousness of the people, the greater will be the possibility of doing something about it. And the more people move away from searching for illusory panaceas and begin to fight for their elementary rights to decent jobs, housing, and medical care, the closer they will come to coping with the real issues.

# *The Alternative to Stagnation*

In his column in *The Nation* of May 10th, Alexander Cockburn, perhaps the U.S. left's most effective journalist/polemicist, writes:

> The success of the Reagan administration so far as news management is concerned—news management being its central preoccupation—is its conditioning of the media to "see" and not to see. To "see" terrorism, but not to see the administration as promoter of terror; to "see" a Reagan economic boom, but not to see the five flat quarters since the fall of 1984 that spell economic failure; to "see" a conservative younger generation, but not to see the omens and realities of new insurgency.

Cockburn goes on to provide striking information on this "new insurgency" gathered from his own experience on university campuses around the country in recent months—information, incidentally, that confirms our own impressions based on less extensive travels. In what follows we would like to elaborate on the second of his two contradictory pairings, that between the illusion of a Reagan economic boom and the reality of economic failure.

It would be easy to fill a whole article with quotations from media stories and pundit pronouncements on the wonderful condition of the U.S. economy in this sixth year of the reign of Ronald Reagan. We confine ourselves to two of the more interesting examples. One is by the usually cautious chairman of the Federal Reserve Board, Paul A. Volcker, often referred to in the business press as the second most powerful person in the nation. Commenting on the Tokyo summit meeting that ended on May 6th, Volcker is quoted in the *New York Times*

This article originally appeared in the June 1986 issue of *Monthly Review*.

of May 7th as saying that this "is a time for optimism, a time for opportunity; after the years of turmoil, there can be years of growth—a good harvest if we do the hard work." And Paul Craig Roberts, a prominent member of Reagan's original team of supply-side economic advisers and now an economics professor at Georgetown, waxes even more lyrical in his regular *Business Week* column of May 12th:

> Economists have been overwhelmed with so much good news that they don't know what to make of it. . . . The economy is in its fourth year of unbroken expansion. Oil prices have collapsed, and the sharp rise in stock prices is predicting an upturn in the long economic expansion. Never has a policy so maligned [i.e., supply-side] been associated with such extraordinary success.

What all these euphoric optimists lack—unfortunately in common with the vast majority of their journalistic and establishment colleagues—is a sense of history, a perspective within which to view the present as part of the continuum that connects the past with the future. In order to provide such a perspective, we present two charts.

Chart 1 shows the official U.S. unemployment rate from 1945 to 1985. The real rate—corrected to take account of so-called discouraged workers and involuntary part-time work—is of course much higher, but the chart undoubtedly gives an accurate picture of the magnitude and timing of changes on the one hand and the overall trend on the other. In general, the changes reflect the ups and downs of the business cycle, while the trend is strongly upward throughout the period. There are two interludes of exceptionally low unemployment, during the Korean and Vietnam wars. As for the business cycle, both successive peaks and troughs are regularly higher than their predecessors.

Chart 2 shows the rate of utilization of industrial capacity from 1965 to 1985. As you would expect, it looks very much like a mirror image of Chart 1: when unemployment increases, capacity utilization declines, and vice versa; and the trends depicted in the two charts go in opposite directions—up in the first, down in the second. These two charts taken together present as clear a picture as one could desire of a stagnant economy

—not one that has ceased to grow but one that on the average falls increasingly short of making full use of the human and material resources available to it.

There is nothing in the experience of the Reagan years to suggest that the economy has broken out of this pattern. Quite the contrary. The present cyclical upswing began in 1983; and now, over three years later (an abnormally long time by historical business-cycle standards), the unemployment rate is still well above—and the capacity utilization rate well below—what they were in 1979 at the previous peak. No one can predict precisely when the present phase of the cycle will end, but there can hardly be a knowledgeable observer who doubts that the next phase will be a downturn or that it is likely to commence sooner rather than later.

But there are special factors that have been at work during these years, and taking them into account can only lead to the conclusion that the underlying condition of the U.S. economy is one not only of stagnation but of steadily deepening stagnation. These factors can be compared to the artificial aids, like pep pills and respirators, that enable mountain climbers to perform better and longer than their natural strength would allow.

The first of those is the huge increase in military spending set in motion by Reagan from the moment he arrived in Washington. The second, which is, of course, closely related, is the unprecedented peacetime deficits the federal government has been running, not only (as orthodox Keynesian theory would prescribe) to help overcome the recession of 1980-82 but throughout the recovery as well. Without these props the recession would undoubtedly have been much longer and the recovery much weaker than they actually were.

But there is another factor of a different kind that needs to be considered in this connection. We have been emphasizing in this space for a long time now that the structural composition of the U.S. economy has been shifting not only from the production of goods to the production of services but also from production (of all kinds) to finance. And this latter shift, while in the most fundamental sense wasteful and parasitical, has had, at least in the short run, significant stimulative effects on

*Chart 1*
*Percent of Labor Force Unemployed*

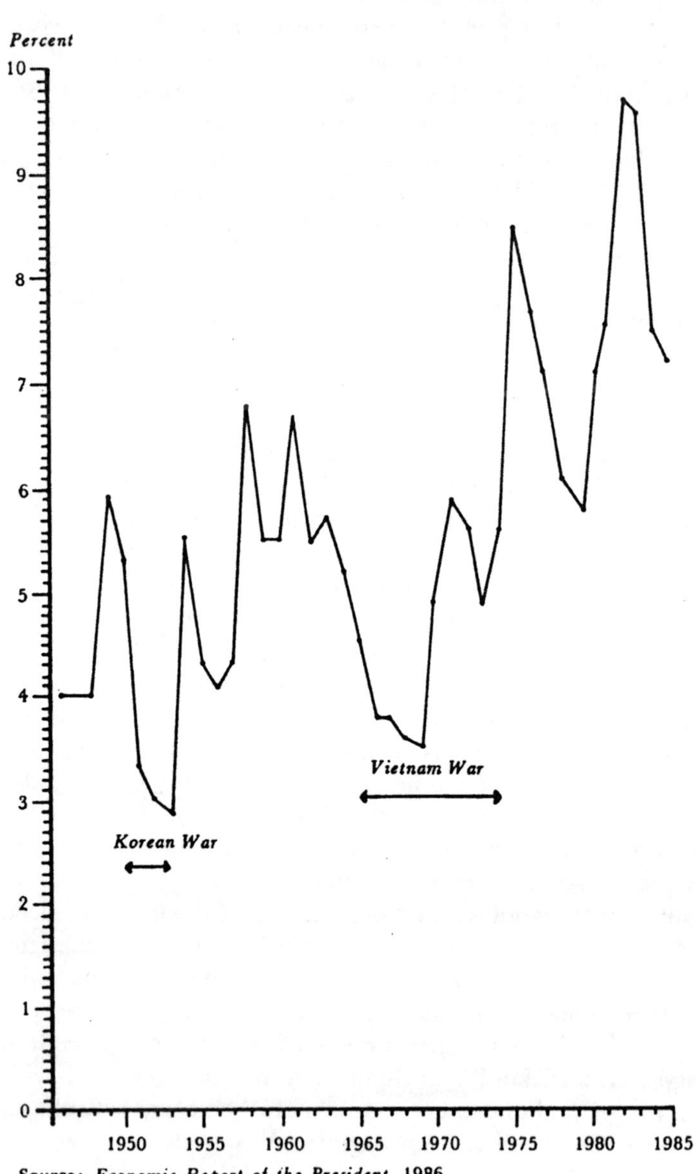


Source: *Economic Report of the President*, 1986

*Chart 2*
*Utilization of Manufacturing Capacity*

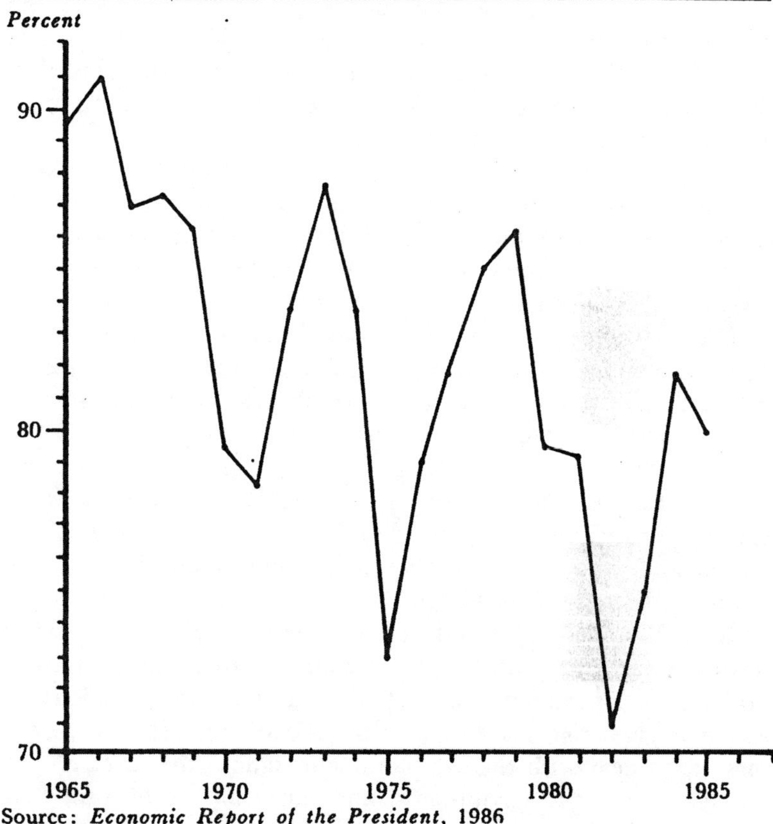


Source: *Economic Report of the President*, 1986

the economy as a whole. How much longer this factor can continue to operate is unclear, though there are already signs of weakness, such as a slump in the market for computers and a sharp curtailment in the construction of new office buildings. But in any case whatever happens in the near future, it would surely make no sense to see this shift from production to finance as a source of continuing economic growth in the future.*

* See "The Strange Recovery of 1983-1984" in this volume, pp. 68-78, where it is shown that the only strong components of investment in the upswing that began in 1983 have been in the sectors that are "for the most part concerned with making money rather than making goods."

All in all, one can hardly avoid the conclusion that the expansionary forces that have been behind the upswing of the last few years—those normal to this phase of the cycle, the military buildup, the continuing deficits, and the structural shift from production to finance—are running out of steam and that the inevitable collapse of the Reaganite illusion is looming more and more ominously on the horizon.

Against this background, what are we to think of the kind of policy debates that command attention in government, in the media, and among analysts of different political persuasions? How are these debates related to the reality of the economic stagnation in which we're stuck and the severe crises that seem certain to emerge as the shaky props that sustain the present relative economic calm weaken and crumble? What kinds of action do our pundits and experts think are needed to improve the prospects for the country's economic future?

Paradoxical though it may seem, the answer to these questions is basically quite simple: there is no relation at all between present realities and ongoing debates about the economic situation and what could or should be done about it. And the reason is that, with negligible exceptions, none of the participants in the debates, regardless of political orientation, starts from a clear and consistent understanding that the underlying problem is stagnation and not the surface manifestations to which it gives rise. As a result, the debates that fill the media these days deal with the symptoms and ignore the disease.

What are these symptoms, and how can we be sure that they are indeed symptoms and not the disease itself? For present purposes it will be sufficient to focus on what are generally perceived to be the most serious problems needing attention: the U.S. trade deficit, and the federal government's budgetary deficit. Do these two deficits, singly or in combination, constitute the main threats to the smooth functioning of the U.S. economy? Or are they merely symptoms of the underlying disease of stagnation?

There are two persuasive reasons for diagnosing them as symptoms. First, in the roughly quarter century of strong growth (the opposite of stagnation) that followed the Second World

War, these problems did not exist. And second, almost all participants in the current economic debates agree that if rapid and sustained growth could somehow be restored, the problems would either disappear or become amenable to relatively easy solutions. Logically, this should lead them directly to the growth/stagnation problem in search of a way out. But, except for a few people on the left, this has not happened. Instead, the nearly unanimous tendency has been to treat the symptoms as causes in the hope of discovering a policy or set of policies calculated to put the country once again on a sustained course of growth.

If, however, our diagnosis is correct, i.e., that stagnation is the disease and deficits its symptoms, then treating the latter as causes is bound to lead into a mass of contradictions and to end in futility and failure.

Consider first the foreign trade deficit, which in the last couple of years has been running at an annual rate of well over $100 billion, with seemingly devastating effects on many U.S. industries and their workers. Foreign competition has been taking over our export markets, and imports have absorbed a larger and larger share of domestic spending on a whole series of products, from steel and autos to TV sets and apparel. Mainstream economic theory teaches that such a massive imbalance in international trade is inherently self-correcting. The outflow of U.S. currency resulting from the deficits should depress the value of the dollar against other currencies, which should make exports cheaper and imports more expensive, and this in turn should lead to a reversal of the adverse trade flows and disappearance of the deficits. But this line of reasoning has been rendered largely obsolete by post-Second World War developments in capitalism's global financial system. Foreign exchange rates which used to be set by trade flows in the manner just described, are now overwhelmingly dominated by the ebb and flow of money capital in which merchandise trade plays only a minor role. In a roundup preparatory for the recent Tokyo summit meeting, the *New York Times* (4 May 1986) gave a concise explanation of this important point:

> Each day, governments watch nervously as a blizzard of round-the-clock trading sets new values for the dollar, the Japanese yen, the German mark, and other major currencies. . . . The foreign exchange market, woven together by modern telecommunications, has grown into an increasingly volatile $150 billion-a-day behemoth that hardly notices national borders. *Just 10 percent of this money directly finances traditional forms of international commerce and investment.* The rest is the trading of currencies by bankers and speculators for whom money has become a commodity, like gold or potatoes. Rumor, hunch, and news play a major role in their decisions about what to sell or buy. (Emphasis added)

In these circumstances the very notion of a self-correcting trade deficit is an anachronism, as the long-lasting U.S. deficit amply attests. As long as foreign capital is eager to come to the United States—whether to take advantage of higher interest rates or because the country is considered a safe haven in a dangerous world—the deficits can continue. And if for any reason foreign capital—possibly joined by sizable chunks from this country as well—decides that it wants to go elsewhere, the result is more likely to be a sudden collapse of the dollar, followed by a global financial crisis, than an improvement in the U.S. trade balance.

It follows that any action to improve the performance of the U.S. economy via the trade balance would have to operate directly on exports and imports rather than indirectly through manipulating foreign exchange rates. And here we meet what has perhaps become the most popular of all approaches to the task of economic revitalization. The problem the country faces, we are told again and again, is that we have lagged behind our foreign rivals with respect to the productive utilization of available human and material resources. *U.S. industry must become more competitive!* This refrain comes not only from the establishment but also from liberal, labor, and even some radical circles. If U.S. industry became more competitive, the trade deficit would presumably disappear, unemployment would be eradicated, and all else would be well.

But how come we are not competitive? Business puts the blame on high wages, the burden of taxes, and government interference. Liberals stress the shortsightedness of corporation executives, inadequate expenditures on research and development, and lack of investment in modern machinery. All sides agree that labor productivity has not been growing fast enough.

The several reasons given for the alleged lack of competitivity are really not very different from each other. Once it is assumed that the primary problem is the relatively high production costs in U.S. manufacturing, the proposed remedies can differ only in emphasis. Even those who claim that profits are too high do not push that argument too far since at the same time they believe that profits should be invested in more modern equipment. In the meantime, the workers get the short end of the stick, since what can be done most quickly to cut costs is to reduce wages and eliminate work rules that union struggles have achieved in the past.

The irony of all the remedies proposed to heighten competitivity is that while they would have little if any impact on the international financial mess, they definitely would intensify the domestic economy's ills. Lower wage incomes depress consumer demand at a time when 20 percent of manufacturing capacity is idle and farm surpluses are piling up in warehouses and silos. Higher productivity of labor, whether by speed-up or labor-saving machinery, throws workers out of jobs at a time of mass unemployment. Thus even if we assume, for the sake of the argument, that some improvement in the trade deficit might (not necessarily would) be achieved through cost-cutting, it by no means follows that there would be any net gain for the economy as a whole.

We turn now to the federal government's budget deficit, which in the current fiscal year is running around $200 billion and is seen by a wide spectrum of opinion as an insuperable obstacle to satisfactory economic growth—or even, in the opinion of not a few observers, as a dire threat to the continuation of the precarious stability of the past few years. The other side of the coin is usually a rosy view of the new economic upsurge that would allegedly emerge once the deficits had been successfully eliminated. Underlying this view is the economic theory that used to be standard in elementary textbooks and is still adhered to by a surprisingly large number of academic and business economists. Growth, the reasoning runs, depends on investment, which in turn depends on saving, hence government deficits absorb savings and inhibit growth. The main point of the "Keynesian revolution" of the 1930s was to refute this theory, and there is no need here to repeat the relevant arguments. Suffice it to say that if there are unemployed workers and idle productive capacity, they can be put to work without any prior saving, and enough fresh saving to match the new investment will be forthcoming from the additional income generated by the increase in economic activity.

Since there has been no lack of unemployment resources in recent years—in fact since the Second World War—the notion that deficits have been sopping up savings needed for investment and growth is obviously fallacious. What actually happens is rather that deficits mobilize funds that would otherwise lie idle (or, in the case of credit, not be created at all) and channel them directly or indirectly into additional demand for goods and services, thus stimulating economic activity. It follows of course that deficits, far from being the cause of stagnation, have been a powerful factor, especially in the Reagan years, keeping stagnation from being much worse than it actually has been.*

If the trade and budgetary deficits are, as we have argued, only symptoms of the disease from which the economy is suffering, we have to ask what can and should be done to tackle the disease itself. How can a fuller and more rational utilization of resources be achieved? How can jobs be provided for the unemployed, food for the hungry, houses for the homeless, adequate health care and income security and a decent environment for all of us?

*We know the answers to these questions, not only from theory but from actual historical experience.*

---

* This is not to imply that deficits are necessarily trouble free. If they are large and financed by borrowing at high interest rates, as has generally been the case during the 1980s, they lead not only to a rapid expansion of the national debt but also to a rising share of federal expenditure being devoted to interest payments. The latter in turn constitutes a redistribution of income from the tax-paying public to the relatively high-income holders of the national debt. This clearly is a process which, if continued long enough, could transform deficits from being a stimulating force into the opposite.

First and most important the nation as a collectivity has to decide that the attainment of these goals is its highest priority to which special interests that now have powers of obstruction and veto must be subordinated. Once this decision has been taken—and assuming it is firmly adhered to—the way forward, if not exactly plain sailing, is at least clearly marked. Major projects like a crash housing program and a comprehensive national health service would have to be drawn up; necessary financing would have to be provided;* arrangements for allocating scarce materials, controlling prices, regulating financial markets, etc., would have to be put in place; and perhaps most important steps would have to be taken to mobilize mass participation in the making and implementation of decisions affecting the welfare of the people. This is of course only a partial listing of what would be needed. But it is worth noting that, apart from special situations, no additional *general* program for dealing with unemployment would be required.

All this may sound very utopian, and in a sense no doubt it is. But not in the sense that it isn't practical or that nothing like it has ever been tried. *In its general design and mode of operation, the program outlined above is basically derived from the U.S. experience in the Second World War.* The difference of course is that then the object was to destroy an enemy, while now it is—or could be—to build a decent society.

Is *this* a utopian project? In time gone by, it doubtless was. Acquiring the capability to provide everyone with what is needed to live a truly human existence is, in a historical sense, an achievement of yesterday. Realizing that capability may of course never happen, and if it does it certainly won't be soon. Is that, however, a reason for not setting it up as a goal, especially now that we know from actual experience that it is a real possibility?

---

* This problem could and should be partly solved by progressive reductions in the military budget; we take it for granted that no new economic course such as we are proposing would be possible except as a counterpart to a radical change in foreign policy of the kind called for in "Questions for the Peace Movement," this volume, pp. 196-208. For the rest, funding should come from higher taxes on corporate profits and deficit financing at interest rates far below those now in force.

But this is not all that needs to be said. The U.S. economy is in a profound state of stagnation, living it up for the moment on artificial stimulants. As we have seen above, the conventional views about what ails the system are partly irrelevant and partly wrong. In these circumstances, the only sensible course is to move toward transforming the system into one that serves human needs. There is no guarantee of success, but surely it is a lot better to struggle for what you want than to resign yourself to what you don't want.

# II

## *Production and Finance*

# *Production and Finance*

In a review of a new book on the problems of the U.S. economy,* Cornell economics professor Alfred E. Kahn, perhaps best known as Jimmy Carter's "inflation fighter," articulates in the briefest and clearest form an important tenet of orthodox economics which is usually taken for granted and left unexpressed. He writes:

> Contrary to popular assumption, speculation in securities, real estate, and commodities, and mergers and acquisitions of existing companies do not waste capital that would otherwise be used for productive investment. All they do is transfer dollars from purchasers to sellers. The authors clearly imply that if these funds had gone instead into new plant and equipment, the result would have been a far more satisfactory rate of economic growth. This is economic nonsense. According to that reasoning, the $66 billion used to purchase stocks in the New York stock exchange this past October alone could instead have more than tripled our acquisition of new plant and equipment! But of course that would have been physically impossible. The point is that these mere purchases and sales of existing assets do not use up real resources (except for the time put into making the transactions). (*New York Times,* Sunday Book Review section, December 12, 1982)

Is this true or isn't it? The answer is that some of it is, some of it isn't, and the conclusion to which it leads is false. By reformulating the statement with a few changes and amendments, we reach the opposite conclusion:

---

This article originally appeared in the May 1983 issue of *Monthly Review.*

* Barry Bluestone and Bennett Harrison, *The Deindustrialization of America: Plant Closings, Community Abandonment, and the Dismantling of Basic Industry* (New York: Basic Books, 1982).

In accordance with popular assumption, speculation in securities, real estate, and commodities, and mergers and acquisitions of existing companies absorb money capital that could otherwise be used for productive investment. Instead of being transferred from purchasers to sellers, they could have gone into buying new plant and equipment, and the result would have been a far more satisfactory rate of economic growth. This is economic common sense. According to that reasoning, the $66 billion used to purchase stocks on the New York stock exchange this past October could have greatly increased our acquisition of new business plant and equipment. With more than 10 percent of the labor force unemployed and more than 30 percent of productive capacity idle, that would have been physically perfectly possible. The point is that purchases and sales of existing assets, while not using up real resources (except for the time put into making the transactions) do provide uses for money capital that otherwise could have been transformed into real capital.

What would (or could) orthodox economists say to this? We're not sure, since they rarely if ever pose the problem in this way. For them money used to buy existing assets is not capital; it is simply a means of circulation which does not impinge on the productive process. This is in keeping with a very old way of looking at the economy, i.e., dividing it into two realms, the "real" and the "monetary," with the latter being treated as a veil which hides the real economic processes. If it can be shown that certain activities pertain only to the monetary realm (like the purchase and sale of existing assets), they can be ruled out as having any influence on the real realm.

The trouble with this approach is that there is in fact no separation between the real and the monetary: in a developed capitalist economy practically all transactions are expressed in monetary terms and require the mediation of actual amounts of (cash or credit) money. Some of these transactions are generated in the process of production (payment of wages, distribution of incomes derived from profits, purchase of means of production and consumer goods) and some are generated by financial transactions (borrowing and lending, purchase and sale of existing assets, etc.). The appropriate analytical separation here is not between real and monetary (all are both real *and* monetary) but between productive and financial. One can thus legitimately distinguish between the underlying productive base of the economy and its financial superstructure (not to be confused of course with the base/superstructure metaphor commonly used in expounding the theory of historical materialism).

In the earlier days of capitalism—roughly prior to the Civil War in the United States—when most production was carried on by small competitive proprietorships or partnerships, the financial superstructure was relatively insignificant and for analytical purposes could be ignored. In those days economists developed the real/monetary distinction as a method of contrasting the way the actual economy functioned and the way a hypothetical barter (moneyless) economy presumably would function. Money was thought of as having been imposed on a natural barter economy, becoming in the process the source of a wide variety of price (as distinct from value) phenomena like inflation, gluts, panics, and later the business cycle.

By the end of the nineteenth century, with the spread of larger and larger corporations as the typical form of business enterprise, the composition of the capitalist economy underwent a qualitative transformation. The issuance of many types and quantities of corporate securities brought in its train the development of organized stock and bond markets, brokerage houses, new forms of banking, and a community of what Veblen called captains of finance who soon rose to the top of the capitalist hierarchy of wealth and power.

In the twentieth century the growth of the financial sector has proceeded apace, both absolutely and relative to the underlying productive sector, most especially in the long post-Second World War boom during which there has occurred a veritable explosion of new kinds of financial institutions and instruments along with speculative activity on an unprecedented scale.

For reasons which need not detain us—and indeed which have never been seriously studied—orthodox economics paid scant attention to this continuing transformation of capitalist economies. To be sure, the rise of large-scale production units was given belated recognition (in the 1930s) in new theories of imperfect or monopolistic competition, but these were focused on individual firms or industries and no attempt was made to extend them to take in the whole economy. Moreover, developments in the field of corporate finance and banking were relegated to the status of "applied economics" having at best a loose and ill-defined relation to the hard core of economic theory (the "neoclassical synthesis") which, apart from a variety of lovingly elaborated refinements, remained pretty much what it had become when Alfred Marshall published the first edition of his *Principles of Economics* in 1890. It is true that the work of Keynes (*A Treatise on Money,* 1930; and *The General Theory of Employment, Interest and Money,* 1936) constituted a partial exception to these generalizations. There is no sign of the real/monetary dichotomy in Keynes, and there are places where he clearly recognizes the distinction between productive and financial sectors (especially in Chapter 15 of *A Treatise on Money* entitled "The Industrial Circulation and the Financial Circulation"). Still, Keynes did not follow up his own leads and never got around to conceptualizing the economy as a whole in terms of the two sectors as a preliminary to exploring their interactions historically as well as analytically. And in this respect, as well as in others, the subsequent development of mainstream economics has been a retreat from the advances pioneered by Keynes in the 1930s.

What has to be understood—and what is missing from the kind of reasoning exemplified by the statement of Alfred Kahn quoted above—is that in modern complex economies, a large and growing part of money capital (i.e., money invested with a view to earning more money) is not directly transformed into productive capital serving as the means by which surplus value is extracted from the productive utilization of labor power. Instead it is used to buy interest-bearing or dividend-yielding financial instruments. It used to be an axiom of orthodox theory that the sellers of these instruments (stocks and bonds) were themselves productive capitalists who would use the proceeds to expand their real capital, handing over to the buyers part of their increased surplus value in the form of interest and dividends. To the extent that this is what actually happens, the money capitalist simply becomes a kind of partner of the productive capitalist.

Nowadays, however, this is very far from what actually happens. Money capitalists are being offered an enormous variety of financial instruments to choose from—stocks and bonds, certificates of deposit, money-market funds, titles to all sorts of assets, options to buy and sell, futures contracts, and so on. There is no presumption, let alone assurance, that money invested in any of these instruments will find its way, directly or indirectly, into real capital formation. It may just as well remain in the form of money capital circulating around in the financial sector, fueling the growth of financial markets which increasingly take on a life of their own.*

In the present state of knowledge it is not possible to define or delineate the financial sector with any accuracy, and perhaps it never will be.** But that it is large and getting larger both absolutely and relatively is clear to any reasonably attentive observer of the economic scene. And these observations can be supported in a general way by readily available statistical data. For example:

- According to data cited by Guy E. Noyes, former vice president and chief economist for Morgan-Guaranty Trust Company (*Morgan-Guaranty Survey,* October 1981), at the end of 1980 debits to demand deposits (i.e., checks written against demand deposits) were running at an annual rate of approximately $68 trillion compared to a Gross National Product of $2.7 trillion. Thus only some 4 percent of payments by check were related to transactions involving the goods and services that compose GNP. "A large volume of transactions, not

---

* The Marxian formula for the productive investment process is M-C-M′—money exchanged for commodities (means of production plus labor power) which are used to produce more valuable commodities which in turn are sold for more money than was originally laid out. The corresponding formula for money capital is M-M′, i.e., money which yields more money without the intervention of a process of production. Marx aptly referred to this as capital in its "most externalized and fetish-like form." (*Capital*, Vol. 3, Kerr ed., p. 459.)

** The difficulty stems in large part from the fact that most of the large corporations which are officially classified as "nonfinancial" are in reality, at least to some extent and often to a substantial extent, engaged in financial operations such as buying and selling securities and other existing assets, borrowing and lending money, etc. They take in large amounts of money (from both productive and financial operations) over and above what they distribute to their stockholders and creditors. In deciding how to invest these funds, they are guided by criteria of profitability, safety, liquidity, etc., which often means that they invest in financial rather than productive assets. They are, in other words, money capitalists as well as productive capitalists.

counted in the 4 percent figure," Noyes explains, "involves intermediate purchases of goods and services—as opposed to final purchases, which is what GNP measures. However, financial payments represent far and away the great bulk of total debits to demand deposits." This does not mean that most of the nation's money is tied up in the financial sector, but it does mean that most of the economy's money *flow* (quantity of money times average number of turnovers in a given unit of time) takes place in the financial sector. Since the rate of turnover is very high in the financial sector, less money is needed to sustain a higher flow of payments. Still, the financial sector does absorb a vast amount of money. It follows of course that any change in the relative profitability of production and finance can quickly send money scurrying from one sector to the other with significant consequences for the way the system functions.

• In 1950 dividends and interest amounted to 8.1 percent of total personal income. By 1982 this had increased to 17.1 percent, a gain of over 110 percent. (*Economic Report of the President,* 1983, pp. 188-89) A major reason for the growth of interest and dividends has been the dramatic rise in interest rates. But that is itself a product of the ballooning financial superstructure which stretches credit to an extreme limit and even beyond the bounds of rational finance.

• Pretax profits of financial corporations averaged 10.9 percent of total corporate profits in 1945-54. This had risen to 15.7 percent by 1975-81, an increase of 44 percent. (*The National Income and Product Accounts of the United States, 1929-76,* pp. 283-84 and *Survey of Current Business,* July 1982, p. 92) The increase in the share of finance would certainly have been greater if it were possible to separate out and count the financial operations of what are officially classified as nonfinancial corporations.

• Employment in "Finance, Insurance and Real Estate" increased from 3.6 million in 1970 to 5.4 million in 1982, a rise of 50 percent. This compares with an increase in total employment in the same period of 26 percent. In other words, in terms of employment the financial sector grew almost twice as fast as the economy as a whole. (*Economic Report of the President,* 1983, p. 205)

The foregoing are evidently no more than indicators or symptoms of long-term trends at work in the U.S. economy; in and of themselves they do not tell us anything about the consequences of the shift away from production and toward finance for the overall functioning of the system. For this we must inquire into the way the two sectors—production and finance—interact with each other.

We have found that the most useful way of pursuing this inquiry focuses on the production and utilization of society's surplus product under conditions of monopoly capitalism. The basic condition for any society's survival and reproduction is the uninterrupted operation of a productive sector which supplies the consumer goods required by the population, plus the producer goods to replace what wears out and (if conditions are favorable) to add to the productive base. In primitive societies there is normally little left over after the people's livelihood has been provided for, so growth is at best slow and often nonexistent. As civilization progresses, labor becomes more productive, the surplus (over and above what is required to maintain the working population) grows, new classes of non-workers emerge (landlords, priests, government functionaries), and faster growth becomes possible. Still, throughout most of human history the surplus remained small and was from time to time reduced or even wiped out in the face of adverse natural conditions, wars, plagues, etc. This is why history seems to move so slowly for so long and why apparently flourishing civilizations decline and fall.

The arrival of capitalism introduces a new dynamic element into the historical process. The rate of increase of labor productivity quickens. As Marx and Engels put it in *The Communist Manifesto,* the "bourgeoisie . . . has created more massive and more colossal productive forces than have all preceding generations together." The surplus product grows by leaps and bounds. During most of the nineteenth century in the countries of advanced capitalism a large part of this growing surplus was plowed back into expanding the productive base, and much of the rest went into nourishing the growth in the numbers and standard of living of the non-working classes. In time, however, these traditional ways of utilizing the surplus proved increasingly inadequate to keep the capitalist machine running at or near full capacity. New science-based technologies and improved forms of organizing the labor process proved to be, in one of Veblen's favorite phrases, "inordinately" productive. One result was, as Veblen noted in a path-breaking study as early as 1904, that the economy tended to slow down and to operate for sustained periods at less than full capacity.* One remedy for this situation, Veblen argued, could be sought "in an increased unproductive consumption of goods," but he was not optimistic about its effectiveness:

> Wasteful expenditure on a scale adequate to offset the surplus productivity of modern industry is nearly out of the question. Private initiative cannot carry the waste of goods and services to nearly the point required by the business situation. Private waste is no doubt large, but business principles, leading to saving and shrewd investment, are too ingrained in the habits of modern men to admit an effective retardation of the rate of saving. Something more to the point can be done, and indeed is being done, by the civilized governments in the way of effectual waste. Armaments, public edifices, courtly and diplomatic establishments, and the like are almost altogether wasteful, so far as bears on the present question. They have the additional advantage that the public securities which represent this waste serve as attractive investment securities for private savings, at the same time that . . . the savings so invested are purely fictitious savings and therefore do not act to lower profits or prices. . . . But however extraordinary this public waste of substance latterly has been, it is apparently altogether inadequate to offset the surplus productivity of the machine industry, particularly when this productivity is seconded by the great facility which the modern business organization affords for the accumulation of savings in relatively few hands. (*Ibid.*, pp. 255-57)

Veblen might have gone on to cite the growth of the financial sector, of which he was one of the earliest and most insightful observers, as an additional offset to the "surplus productivity of modern industry." The reason he didn't is probably that at the time he was writing *The Theory of Business Enterprise* in the

* "It might even be a tenable generalization . . . to say that for a couple of decades past the normal condition of industrial business has been a mild but chronic state of depression. . . . Seasons of easy times, 'ordinary prosperity,' during this period are pretty uniformly traceable to specific causes extraneous to the process of industrial business proper." (*The Theory of Business Enterprise*, pp. 184, 251.)

first years of the present century the financial sector, in a purely quantitative sense, was still quite small. It is interesting to note that Baran and Sweezy, in *Monopoly Capital* (1966), also failed to focus on finance, along with the sales effort and government spending, as a major absorber of surplus, although they had much less reason than Veblen for the oversight. Be that as it may, there is certainly no excuse for continuing to ignore this role of finance after the fantastic explosion of the financial sector which characterized the 1960s and 1970s.

If a capitalist economy worked in the manner assumed by the textbook models, there would be no reason for the development of a distinct financial sector. All incomes would be paid out by productive enterprises in the form of wages, salaries, dividends, interest, and rent; and all incomes would be spent on consumer goods or on means of production serving to expand the productive base of the economy. Savings would be directly invested in or loaned at interest to productive enterprises, and credit would be limited to the modest role of facilitating commercial transactions and economizing on the need for cash.

With the coming of corporations all this gradually changed. The original purpose of the corporate form was to allow a number of investors to go into an enterprise together without each of them running the risk of losing his or her entire fortune. The matter is often presented as though this is really only an extended partnership with each participant actually owning a piece of the productive assets in question. But this is not so. The corporation itself owns the real assets, and the participants own only shares in the corporation—pieces of paper embodying specified legal rights (to vote for directors, receive dividends when declared, acquire a pro rata share of assets in case the corporation is liquidated, etc.). The difference between owning real assets and owning a bundle of legal rights may at first sight seem unimportant, but this is emphatically not the case. It is in fact the root of the division of the economy into productive and financial sectors.

Corporations can of course sell their assets, wholly or in part. Shareholders on the other hand can only sell their pieces of paper. In the absence of an organized market, this is not easy, as many early corporate shareowners discovered. But even before the rise of the corporation, organized securities markets existed, most notably those handling government bonds and to a lesser extent the shares of banks and insurance companies. As the volume of new corporate securities swelled in the closing decades of the nineteenth century, the established dealers and brokers—a good example was J. P. Morgan who got his start as a financier to the Northern government during the Civil War—were more than anxious to extend their activities to include these new types of securities.

It was in this fashion that corporate securities acquired the attribute of liquidity—instant convertibility into cash—which the physical assets of corporations by their very nature could never have. And once this stage had been reached, the way was open for a proliferation of financial instruments and markets which, so far at any rate, has proved to be literally unlimited. A crucial step in this development was the determination by state legislatures and the courts that corporations had the power not only to issue their own securities but also to own the securities of other corporations. Thus was born the holding company, a corporation whose purpose is to own the securities of other companies. Given this possibility, corporations could be piled on top of other corporations in a theoretically endless chain, with the aggregate number and volume of corporate securities growing in step and without any addition to the underlying productive base at the bottom of the pyramid.

This is not the place to detail the various other ways in which the financial sector, once established on a solid independent basis, expanded its size and its influence. Buying and selling securities on credit, the development of options and futures markets, the multiplication of specialized financial intermediaries, orchestration of corporate mergers and acquisitions—all these and more have been part of the build-up which has resulted in the huge financial sector which looms so large on the present-day economic scene.

What, then, is the nature of the interrelation between the productive and the financial sectors? Clearly the financial sector does not itself produce anything with significant use value. On the other hand it does use up a lot of real resources: the nearly 5.4 million employed in this sector (see p.98 above) presumably consume on the average as much as (and perhaps even more than) employees in the rest of the economy; banks seem to need fancier buildings than most businesses; a very substantial part of the output of the hi-tech industries (computers, communication equipment, etc.) certainly goes to the financial sector. In Veblen's terminology quoted above, the financial sector evidently does its part to offset the surplus productivity of modern industry. Nor is the demand which it directly generates for consumer goods and means of production the full extent of its contribution in this respect. Recent years, and even more dramatically the last nine months, have shown that the financial sector can prosper while the productive sector continues to stagnate.* When this happens, the favorable impact of the financial sector on the productive sector is not limited to the increased demand for the latter's products created by more employment and greater profits in the financial sector. There is also the indirect effect of an increase in the value of financial assets held by households and businesses throughout the economy. The *Morgan-Guaranty Survey* for March estimates that "the value of consumer-held stocks, bonds, and liquid assets rose more than $500 billion in the last half of 1982," obviously wholly a result of activity in the financial sector. This should have some stimulating effect on consumer demand, though in the present overall condition of the economy this may show up more in slowing a decline than in registering an increase.

What about the outlook for the period ahead? Can this seemingly contradictory coexistence of a prosperous and expanding financial sector and a stagnant production sector continue? It is probably safe to say that in the long run the answer is no. But this doesn't help much since no one can define the long run, and in the meantime capitalist enterprises are for the most part constrained, whether they like it or not, to make decisions on the basis of the immediate outlook.

In the productive sector, with demand stagnant and nearly a third of productive capacity lying idle, this means trimming

---

* Between August 1982 and the end of February this year the New York Stock Exchange composite index went up 35.7 percent, while industrial production and profits of nonfinancial corporations were both declining.

costs of production (especially by firing workers and cutting wages) and limiting investment to unavoidable maintenance and replacement—a perfect recipe for perpetuating stagnation. In the financial sector things are different. There is plenty of money available (cash plus unused credit), and hunger for profits added to competitive pressures drives all financial enterprises to put as much of it as possible to work. This generates an upward tendency in the price of financial instruments which in turn sparks a speculative psychology which comes to pervade the financial community and to provide its own justification.

From a structural point of view, i.e., given the far-reaching independence of the financial sector discussed above, financial inflation of this kind can persist indefinitely. But is it not bound to collapse in the face of the stubborn stagnation of the productive sector? Are the two sectors really that independent? Or is what we are talking about merely an inflationary bubble that is bound to burst as many a speculative mania has done in the past history of capitalism?

No assured answer can be given to these questions. But we are inclined to the view that in the present phase of the history of capitalism—barring a by no means improbable shock like the breakdown of the international monetary and banking system—the coexistence of stagnation in the productive sector and inflation in the financial sector can continue for a long time. The reason is that the underlying attitudes of the capitalist class, especially in the United States, are dominated by a set of expectations deeply rooted in the history of the capitalist system. Capitalist ideology takes for granted that the *normal* state of the economy is prosperity based on vigorous growth. Deviations from this norm—so the argument goes—are temporary and bound to be reversed. This holds not only for the recessions/depressions of the ordinary business cycle but also for the longer periods of stagnation which are supposed to come along every 50 years or so (hence the growing popularity in the business press of theories of the so-called long-wave cycle). We are in such a period now, according to this view, and it is due to last pretty much through the 1980s and to be followed by a new long upswing in the 1990s and after.

As long as capitalists really believe this (or something similar)—and we think there is no doubt that they do—it provides a reasonable explanation for the kinds of behavior which characterize the productive and financial capitalists respectively. Those who are entrenched in the productive sector can only batten down the hatches (mostly at the expense of labor) and wait for the new long-term upswing to begin. Those who operate in the financial sector on the other hand can rationally (so it seems to them) value their pieces of paper at what they presumably will be worth after the upswing gets under way. Hence stagnation in the productive sector and inflation in the financial sector.

As MR readers know, we regard the 50-year cycle as ideology in the bad sense of the term, i.e., a myth which serves to rationalize capitalist interests. The norm of mature capitalism is stagnation, not vigorous growth. In the absence of powerful extraneous stimuli, of which there are no present signs anywhere on the horizon, the stagnation drags on and, except for occasional zigs and zags, feeds on itself. If this is a correct diagnosis, the U.S. capitalist class, like the rest of the American people, is in for a rude awakening some time down the road. But whether this will occur in the "natural" course of events, or whether a severe shock such as might be administered by an international financial panic will intervene and set events on a new course—these are questions to which no sensible answers can be given in advance. In the meanwhile we must not be surprised if the strange *pas de deux* being enacted these days by the productive and financial sectors continues for a considerable time yet.

# *The Federal Deficit: The Real Issues*

Behind the fuss and fury over current U.S. budget deficits looms a crucial paradox that frustrates our economic pundits, financiers, and politicos.

On the one hand, the United States has been relying more and more on budget deficits to keep the economy afloat. Washington has operated with red ink in 23 of the past 25 years, thus providing a prop to an economy that has been sliding into stagnation during much of the post-Second World War period. One of the most astute and outspoken business economists, Albert Wojnilower of the First Boston Corporation, hit the nail on the head when he said: "I think the budget deficit is what stands between us, is a large part of what has stood and will be standing between us and a depression with a capital D." (*Barron's,* November 8, 1982)

On the other hand, the stimulation generated by unending and ever more red ink is self-limiting. Deficits piled on top of deficits provide fuel for new inflationary spirals and help sustain high interest rates; and at the same time they set in motion forces that eventually arrest growth and lead to a new business decline. In short, today's capitalism finds itself on the horns of a dilemma: it can't live without deficits and it can't live with them.

This impasse has led to a great deal of confusion and even more obfuscation. Unable or unwilling to face up to the real causes behind the unending flow of red ink, the conventional wisdom has turned on the deficit as the root of all evil. Capitalists don't invest, interest rates are high, prices go up—all because of the deficit. The truth lies elsewhere: growing and per-

This article originally appeared in the April 1984 issue of *Monthly Review.*

sistent deficits are not the cause but the product of stagnating investment, high interest rates, and the inflationary pressures of monopoly capital.

In a period of vigorous economic growth, budget deficits tend to be balanced by surpluses. Deficits are normally produced by recessions, since tax collections contract as unemployment grows and profits fall while expenditures rise to meet increased unemployment benefits and welfare payments. This process is reversed during recoveries, with resultant budgetary surpluses. This wave-like motion of government finance characterized the early stages of the long period of post-Second World War prosperity. Deficit years alternated with surplus years from 1947 through the 1950s. But that changed as the wave of prosperity began to taper off in the 1960s. Deficits, swollen by spending for the Vietnam war, began to be the order of the day. Still the deficit remained relatively small.

As stagnation set in during the 1970s, however, a new pattern emerged: deficits not only became a fixed feature of the U.S. economy but kept growing in importance as a stimulating factor in the upward as well as the downward phases of the business cycle. And it was in the 1970s that the financial community and the academic experts began to focus on the deficit as the alibi for the economic slowdown. Private investment (and hence economic growth) was constrained, it was and still is claimed, because savings were insufficient to finance both the deficit and capital investment. The deficit was supposed to be crowding out the supply of funds that would otherwise be used for capacity expansion and new jobs. But this was putting the cart before the horse. It was, in fact, the faltering of capital investment that set the stage for ever larger deficits and other government policies designed to fill the gap in effective demand.

The story is told in Table 1. The key to what happened is the steady decline in the rate of growth of investment in residential construction, nonresidential structures, and producers' durable equipment, as shown in column 2. From one five-year period to the next the rate of growth in investment declined markedly. And as the investment slowed down, the deficit (adjusted for price increases) kept rising rapidly (column 3).

In the 1960s capital investment was still strong and the deficit as a percent of fixed investment (column 4) was small.

*Table 1*
*Federal Deficit and Capital Investment*
*(in billions of 1972 dollars)*

| | Fixed Investment | | Federal Deficit | |
|---|---|---|---|---|
| | *Annual average* (1) | *Percent change from preceding period* (2) | *Annual average* (3) | *Deficit as percent of fixed investment (3) ÷ (1)* (4) |
| 1960-64 | $111.0 | — | $ 2.6 | 2.3% |
| 1965-69 | 148.4 | +33.7% | 3.5 | 2.4 |
| 1970-74 | 177.9 | +19.9 | 14.0 | 7.9 |
| 1975-79 | 197.8 | +11.2 | 31.2 | 15.8 |
| 1980-83 | 214.2 | + 8.3 | 51.9 | 24.2 |

*Note:* Fixed investment includes investment in residential construction, nonresidential structures, and producers' durable equipment.

*Source: Economic Report of the President,* February 1984. The deficit data are for calendar years adjusted to be consistent with the national income and product accounts (Table B-76) deflated by the implicit price deflators for government purchases of goods and services. The fixed investment data are from Table B-2.

But note how rapidly that percentage kept mounting during the 1970s and thus far in the 1980s, reaching over 24 percent in the last four years. The implication of Table 1 is quite different from the current illusion that the deficit is "crowding out" investment. The real relationship is the opposite: the ever-growing deficit was not able to arrest the course of stagnation. And the pressures brought about by stagnation in turn were such that an expanding deficit became more and more essential to forestall a major depression.

But "crowding out" is not the only dire consequence for which deficits are the alleged cause: they are also routinely being blamed for high interest rates. We will show below that the basic cause of the upward trend in interest rates has an entirely different origin. This is not to deny that deficits do in fact contribute to sustaining high interest rates, but the really significant relationship between the two variables runs in the opposite direction, i.e., from the level of interest rates to the size of the deficit. The steady diet of deficits has produced a phenomenal rise in the accumulated federal debt—from $382.6 billion in

1970 to $1,381.9 billion in 1983, or a 261 percent expansion. A large portion of this debt is in short-term securities that must be continuously refinanced at ever higher interest rates. The combination of an exploding debt and mounting interest rates has made "the cost of servicing the U.S. debt the fastest rising component of government spending." (*Business Week,* January 16, 1984)

To appreciate the full significance of the growing interest burden, it is worth noting that the increase in interest payments on the federal debt since President Reagan took office exceeds all of his administration's budget cuts in health, education, and welfare programs. This point was highlighted in a *New York Times* (February 5, 1984) report on the 1985 budget:

> Under Mr. Reagan's 1985 budget, sent to Congress this week, the government would pay $116.1 billion in interest on the debt, or $47.4 billion more than the amount spent for the same purpose in 1981. The Congressional Budget Office estimates legislative changes since January 1981 have reduced Federal spending on social welfare programs $29.6 billion below what it would otherwise have been in 1985.
>
> For the four-year period from 1982 through 1985, the Congressional Budget Office estimated the cumulative total of all savings in social welfare programs at $110 billion. That is less than the $124 billion increase in spending on interest payments required over the same four-year period. Thus, savings in domestic programs have been swallowed up by higher interest costs.

The data on interest payments in the budget are given in Table 2. There we can see that these payments on the federal debt rose five-fold in the past ten years—from $21.7 billion in 1975 to $108.6 billion in 1984. This growth has far exceeded the rate of increase in total expenditures. A comparison between the two is made in the last column of the table, where it can be seen that interest payments as a percent of federal expenditures almost doubled, from 6.6 percent in 1975 to 12.4 percent in the current fiscal year. This trend is bound to continue if present policies are unchanged. With projected deficits in the range of $200 billion a year, the Congressional Budget Office estimates that the federal debt will climb another $1,000 billion in five years. Assuming interest rates of 10 percent, that would mean

*Table 2*
*The Government Interest Burden*

| *Fiscal year* | *Federal expenditures* | *Net interest payments on the federal debt* | *Interest as a percent of expenditures* |
|---|---|---|---|
| | — *Billions of dollars* — | | |
| 1975 | 328.8 | 21.7 | 6.6% |
| 1976 | 370.7 | 25.2 | 6.8 |
| 1977 | 411.2 | 28.4 | 6.9 |
| 1978 | 450.4 | 33.5 | 7.4 |
| 1979 | 495.6 | 40.6 | 8.2 |
| 1980 | 576.5 | 50.7 | 8.8 |
| 1981 | 668.1 | 67.7 | 10.1 |
| 1982 | 740.0 | 82.2 | 11.1 |
| 1983 | 816.4 | 90.6 | 11.1 |
| 1984[a] | 875.5 | 108.6 | 12.4 |

[a] Estimate
*Source: Economic Report of the President,* February 1984. Table B-76.

an interest burden in excess of $200 billion a year (more than the government now spends on social security). In other words, if present trends continue, the interest share of the budget may before long reach 25 percent—a doubling of that ratio in the next five years as compared with a doubling in the preceding ten years.

But are the high interest rates that impose such a heavy burden on the budget inevitable? What happened during the Second World War proves beyond a shadow of doubt that they are not. In the war years from 1942 to 1945, the average annual deficit was 23 percent of Gross National Product, and of course that was a time when available economic resources were stretched to the limit. Yet the interest rate on three-month Treasury bills in those years was less than one-half of 1 percent, and on highest-grade corporate bonds it was less than 3 percent. Thus far in the 1980s, in contrast, the average annual deficit has been only 3.8 percent of GNP, and there has been plenty of slack in the economy (at least 10 million unemployed and a quarter of manufacturing capacity idle). Yet the average interest rate has been over 11 percent on three-month U.S. Treasury bills and 13 percent on AAA corporation bonds.

Why this startling contrast? The fundamental reason is a whole series of changes in government policy. The Roosevelt administration was determined to minimize the cost of carrying the war debt, and to this end Federal Reserve and Treasury policies were concentrated on keeping the interest rate below a set maximum. The practices of postwar administrations, to put it mildly, have been just the opposite. Credit expansion and a burgeoning financial sector played a unique role in prolonging the postwar wave of prosperity.* But the reforms of the banking system enacted during the 1930s often stood in the way. Washington, bending to the pressures of the financial community, gradually dismantled the apparatus created by the New Deal to control the banking system and to keep a lid on interest rates. With the barriers removed, interest rates soared to amazingly new heights, and these higher levels became embedded in the financial system.

The upshot of the mushrooming financial sector, supported by the progressive deregulation of the credit system, can be seen in the accompanying chart that depicts the course of interest rates on three-month Treasury bills from 1945 to 1983. The wavelike motion of the line on the chart reflects cyclical changes in the demand for credit. But what is noteworthy is the underlying upward trend. While each recession brings down interest rates, the ensuing recovery more than compensates for the preceding decline and leads to a new peak. Behind this pattern is a combination of factors: an unrelenting expansion of debt, a proliferation of financial institutions, and the removal of government controls.

The policies implemented by the New Deal forbade interest payments by banks on insured checking accounts. Furthermore, the Federal Reserve Board and the Federal Deposit Insurance Corporation set maximum rates of interest that banks could pay on insured savings deposits. The reason for these regulations was to prevent a recurrence of the banking disaster of the 1930s. Fierce competition during the 1920s had led banks to keep on raising interest payments to attract deposits. But to earn enough to cover these interest payments and still make a

* See "Production and Finance" in this volume, pp. 93-105.

*Chart 1*
*Interest Rate on 3-Month U.S. Treasury Bills*

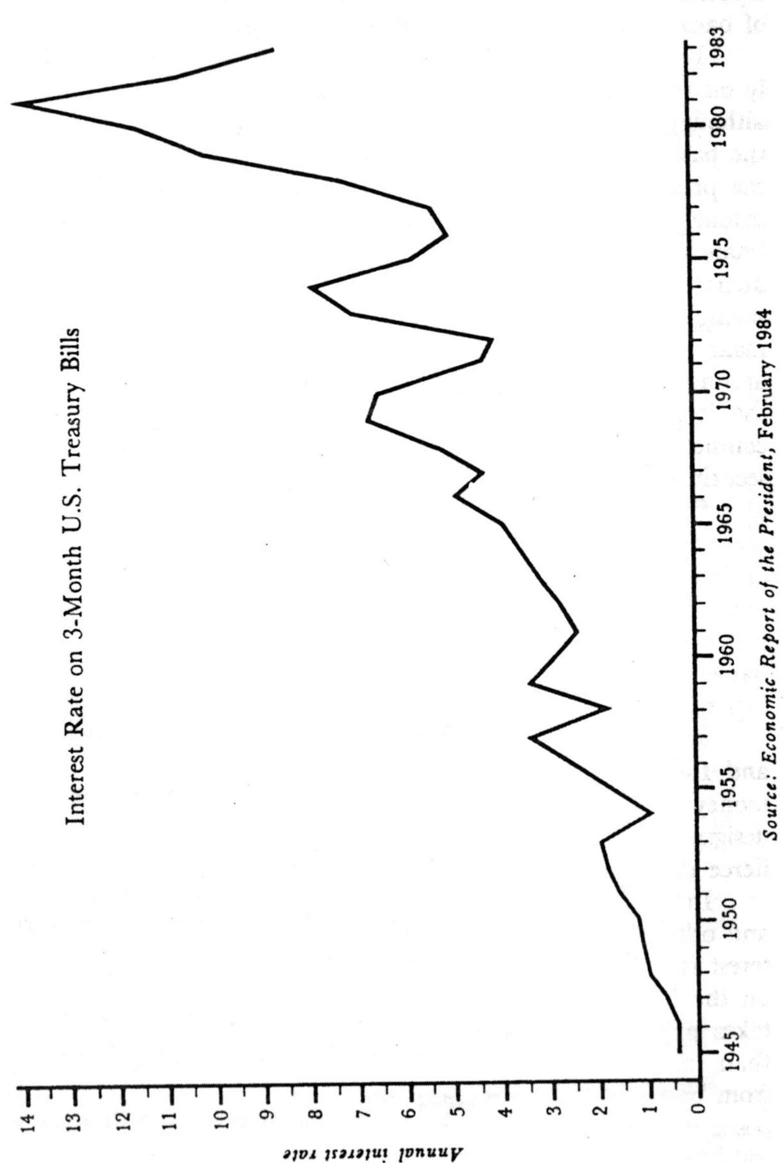

profit, the banks extended risky high-interest loans. The onset of the 1930s depression produced a multiplicity of defaults, especially by the high-risk borrowers, and a consequent inability of banks to return depositors' funds.

The memory of the resulting banking crisis weighed heavily on the minds of government officials and Congress. Hence, although controls were eased shortly after the end of the war, the basic New Deal laws and practices remained in effect. But the pressures of a ballooning financial system eventually broke through the barriers. The number and type of unregulated financial firms multiplied. Seeking to compete by offering higher interest rates, they drew deposits away from commercial and savings banks. The insured banks, faced with a loss of profit-making opportunities, counteracted by devising ways of getting around government restrictions. For example, they introduced the "repurchase agreement" instrument, which enables banks to compete for funds from large depositors by selling government securities in their portfolios with a guarantee to buy them back at a fixed time and price, thus assuring an attractive return to those who in this way lend money to the banks under the guise of buying securities. These contracts were not subject to the Fed's reserve requirements, nor, more importantly, to the Fed's interest-ceiling regulations. Another innovation was the negotiable certificate of deposit issued in large denominations and at higher interest rates than the maximum set for savings deposits.

What followed was a flow of deposits and investments back and forth from one financial firm to another and from one money market instrument to another. Hence despite regulations designed to restrict competition and reckless expansion of credit, fierce rivalry ensued.

In this way the imperatives of competition drive the banks and other financial institutions to play the game by raising interest rates to attract funds and then charging still higher rates on the loans they make. Here is a simple illustration of what takes place. A money market fund offers higher interest rates than can be obtained at a bank. Deposits then begin to move from banks to the money fund. In order to replace the lost deposits, the banks offer large certificates of deposit (CDs) with still higher interest rates. The money market fund then buys the

CDs, enabling them to hold on to their investors. This kind of circular flow of funds both swells the financial sector and at the same time keeps the interest rate jumping from one peak to another.

All this has been happening with Washington's open or tacit approval, often given under the threat of an imminent financial collapse. The growing reliance of the business community on debt and the aggressive expansion of the financial sector have given rise to a number of near-crises in financial markets. Sometimes these were caused by a temporary drying-up of the supply of credit when corporations needed to continue borrowing to service past debts and to keep their heads above water. There were also times when bankruptcies or near-bankruptcies contained the potential of a chain reaction that would cause disaster in financial markets, as for example Penn Central in 1970; Franklin National Bank and a number of real estate investment trusts in 1974; the Hunt Brothers, First Pennsylvania Bank, and Chrysler in 1980. At each of these critical junctures, the Fed acted to save the banks by feeding funds to them to improve their liquidity, liberalizing interest rate restrictions, and legitimizing the devices already adopted by banks to get around regulations.

Finally, Congress put its stamp of approval on deregulation, for all practical purposes lifting whatever barriers to competition and climbing interest rates remained. As a consequence of the Depositary Institution Deregulation and Monetary Control Act of 1980, interest-rate ceilings were removed on all bank deposits except for accounts less than $2,500 maturing within 31 days. The Garn-St. Germain Depositary Institutions Act of 1982 permitted banks to open money market accounts competitive with money market mutual funds. The door has thus been fully opened to the competitive struggle over the entire spectrum of financial firms—the kind of rivalry that stimulates the expansion of credit and keeps interest rates in the stratosphere.

Set against this history, it certainly makes no sense to identify the government deficit as the culprit. This is not to deny that financing present and contemplated deficits will contribute to sustaining high interest rates and may help push them to even higher levels. But the underlying process is at work regardless of deficits. At bottom the reason for the highest interest rate levels in the past century is located in the financial superstructure that has emerged in recent decades—one that evolved with the collusion, if not the encouragement, of past and present administrations, Democratic as well as Republican.

Washington not only helped remove the lid on interest rates but has gone along with an explosion of speculative markets and activity that are exercising an important influence on the structure of interest rates. This upsurge in speculation is summarized in Table 3. Back in 1960 the buying and selling of

*Table 3*
*Speculative Markets: Futures Trading*

| | Number of Contracts (in millions) | | | | |
|---|---|---|---|---|---|
| | *1960* | *1976* | *1981* | *1982* | *1983* |
| Commodities | 3.9 | 29.3 | 53.8 | 51.2 | 64.6 |
| Precious metals | — | 7.2 | 15.7 | 28.8 | 22.6 |
| Financial instruments | — | .2 | 22.9 | 18.8 | 28.1 |
| Foreign currency | — | .2 | 6.1 | 8.7 | 11.9 |
| Stock indexes | — | — | — | 4.9 | 12.8 |
| Total | 3.9 | 36.9 | 98.5 | 112.4 | 140.0 |

*Source:* Releases of Futures Industry Association.

contracts involving bets on the course of future prices was confined to commodities, primarily such agricultural products as soybeans, grains, and livestock. The total number of such contracts traded in the traditional futures markets amounted to 3.9 million in 1960. But that was peanuts compared to what has been happening in the past ten years. In the second half of the 1970s, in a context of deepening stagnation, futures markets were established in precious metals, foreign currency, and financial instruments, to be followed in early 1980 by contracts on future fluctuations in the average of stock prices. The phenomenal outburst of speculation can be seen in the almost fourfold increase in the number of futures contracts traded, from 36.9 million in 1976 to 140 million in 1983.

Especially noteworthy is the flowering of the futures market in financial instruments. The latter include Treasury bonds, negotiable CDs, and Government National Mortgage Association (Ginnie Mae) mortgage-based securities. The technical differences among these need not concern us here. What is relevant is that they are all vehicles for gambling on the future course of interest rates. The amount of money advanced by speculators is relatively small because of the narrow margins required. But the volume of financial instruments traded and subject to speculative fluctuations is enormous. Thus the value of the 28.1 million contracts turned over in 1983 on financial-instrument futures amounts to over $7 trillion, or close to $28 billion a day. In these circumstances the question of how much deficits influence interest rates is removed from the realm of objective analysis of supply and demand factors and transferred to that of the subjective fantasies of speculators. Similarly, the "crowding out" issue takes on a different dimension. According to *Business Week* (September 15, 1980):

> Swarms of U.S. and foreign investors, both institutional and individual, are rushing into futures because of the small margin required and because of the variety of contracts being traded. By doing so, they are shifting their dollars away from the traditional capital-formation mainstream—out of investment and into something close to out-and-out gambling.

The U.S. economy, it seems, has reached a stage where, to use Keynes' image, production has become the bubble on speculation rather than speculation being the bubble on production.

Practically all recent discussion of the alleged evils of deficits leaves out what really matters, i.e., the origin and purposes of the deficits. The Reagan-designed deficit mess stems from the simultaneous reduction of taxes on the rich and a monstrous expansion of military spending. At the same time, welfare expenditures have been severely reduced on the pretext that the deficit needs to be contained. The result is a more regressive distribution of income, a dismemberment of New Deal reforms, and a wasting of human and economic resources—not to mention the worldwide devastation that the expanded weaponry can wreak.

But this is not the way it has to be. Deficits can be socially useful and constructive if incurred to provide jobs for the unemployed, strengthen health and education services, construct decent housing, protect the weak and elderly, and restore the country's disintegrating infrastructure.

But, we shall be asked, wouldn't a benign deficit also contain the potential for renewed inflation and turmoil in financial markets? Perhaps, if nothing else were done. The fear of deficits rests on the implicit assumption that everything else in the economic system is sacrosanct and only deficits are subject to manipulation. Private ownership of profit-making banks, a huge financial superstructure, and aggressive expansion of these institutions are taken as part of the natural order of things. Similarly it is implicitly assumed that the enormous waste of credit to finance mergers of large corporations, to promote tax-avoidance schemes, and to fuel speculation is unavoidable.

What is true is that the contradictions of capitalism cannot be resolved, let alone eliminated, without transforming the system from one of production for profit to one of production for use. But this doesn't mean that all reforms are impossible. Much depends on circumstances and on the understanding, organization, and militancy of the vast majority of the people who are victimized by the present system. The rich historical experience accumulated during the periods of the Great Depression and the Second World War has demonstrated that public control over finance and prices can minimize many of the complications incident to large budgetary deficits. But for this the mass of the population would have first to free itself from the blinders imposed by the dominant ideology and unite to fight for its own interests.

# *Money Out of Control*

> The illusions concerning the miraculous power of the credit and banking system, as nursed by some socialists, arise from a complete lack of familiarity with the capitalist mode of production and the credit system as one of its forms.
>
> Karl Marx, *Capital,* Vol. III

Milton Friedman and other prominent monetarists claim that the cause of the Great Depression's length and severity was the failure of the Federal Reserve Board to act properly. They argue further that Fed policies have greatly contributed to every recession since then and have also operated to promote inflation. And conservatives are not alone in judging the Fed to be a prime source of our economic ills. Although liberals scorn monetarist theory and reject the biases of the right, they nevertheless also believe that tight-money policies of the Fed have been largely to blame for postwar recessions, especially those since the late 1960s. And among radicals as well there is a tendency to fall in line with the notion that manipulation of the money supply plays a decisive role in the business cycle. Popular control of the Fed is therefore advocated by some radicals as a panacea—one that could presumably create jobs, revive sick industries, and generally guard against economic calamities.

What is astonishing about this widespread delusion is its persistence in view of the historical record. Business declines,

This article originally appeared in the December 1984 issue of *Monthly Review*.

supposedly generated in the United States by the monetary authorities, have occurred elsewhere as well. Not one of the world's capitalist countries—whether run by socialists, liberals, or conservatives—has been able to escape the business cycle. An assortment of corrective devices have been tried, central bankers have come and gone, yet postwar recessions have kept on recurring with increasing severity, accompanied by the spread of stagnation throughout the capitalist world. Is this because of uniform incompetence or ill-will of all central bankers? Or is it the other way around, that depressions and stagnation are inherent in profit-directed societies, so much so that monetary and other government officials simply don't have the power to prevent them? By now, the answer to this question should be obvious enough.

We are not implying that the Federal Reserve System is unimportant. It does in fact play a very significant role, but it does so within definite limits. One of its most important activities these days is to try to prevent an overstretched debt structure from bursting at the seams. When the debt burdens of industry are especially heavy, depressions contain the seeds of financial crisis. Sales dry up, cash becomes short, debts cannot be repaid, and banks become increasingly vulnerable. While the Fed cannot prevent an industrial depression, it can in many instances halt the onset of a derivative *domestic* financial crisis. Furthermore, financial panics can crop up, independently of business depressions, as a result of excessive speculation or the failure of one or more major financial or nonfinancial corporations. Here too the Fed can do something, and if it steps in quickly and vigorously enough it may be able to stave off the threatened panic. The recent rescue operation of Continental Illinois Bank is a case in point.

While the rescue function of the Fed is rarely a subject of debate, what does stir controversy is the Fed's money-management function. Experience has taught, as Walter Bagehot put it many years ago in his famous *Lombard Street,* that "money does not manage itself." The demand for money fluctuates during the year due to seasonal factors (e.g., Christmas shopping, tax-payment periods), and it will differ from year to year for a variety of reasons, not the least of which are the alternating phases of the business cycle. Centralized management is therefore needed in order to ensure a flexible money supply—one that will adequately meet changing business conditions.

It is this central money-management function that has become the source and stimulus for the illusions that have grown up around the Fed's supposed omnipotence. According to the conventional wisdom, what the Fed does determines the size of the money supply. The reality is quite different. The main creators of money in modern capitalist economies are the banks. Basically, it is the expansion and contraction of credit issued by the banks that determine the money supply. The central bank's role is essentially secondary: in the final analysis, its operations are directed to accommodating the needs of the banking system and to preventing a collapse of financial markets. Our reason for saying this will become clearer if we begin by reviewing the origins of the Federal Reserve System.

### The Rise of the Federal Reserve System

The impetus for the establishment of the Federal Reserve came from the urgent need to avoid the kind of serious breakdowns of the financial system that had become familiar features of the U.S. economy during the late nineteenth and early twentieth centuries. In the course of the post-Civil War reconstruction years, the United States embarked on a process of vigorous industrialization. Tied up with this new burst of economic energy was the emergence of the new stage of monopoly capital and the country's emergence on the world stage as an exporter of manufactures and a colonial power. But none of these changes came smoothly. They were accompanied by wild bursts of speculation and alternating waves of expansion and stagnation.

It soon became clear that the decentralized and unregulated money and banking system inherited from the earlier period threatened to stifle economic growth. Severe financial crises broke out during this era of rampant development, most notably in 1873, 1893, and 1907. This last panic, following an intense bout of speculative fever, was especially virulent. First, the important Knickerbocker Trust Company had to close its doors;

then other trust companies, and banks that had close relations with trust companies, failed. The practice in those years was for country banks to keep their reserves in New York. These reserves in turn were lent by New York bankers to stock market and other speculators. As panic spread, the out-of-town banks sought in vain to withdraw their New York deposits. Bank failures in the money center and the inability of even the still-operating banks to pay out all withdrawal demands of the country banks led to a period when monetary payments virtually came to a halt.

The severity of the 1907 panic finally led to decisive action. A Monetary Commission was set up by Congress to develop a plan for a more rational money system, rational of course meaning how best to service the business community; that is, how to avoid periodic shortages of money and runs on banks leading to panics and economic breakdowns. The more deep-seated irrationalities of the business system—its speculative excesses, waste, misallocation of resources, and creation of poverty and insecurity—were of course not addressed. The conventional diagnosis of the prevailing financial difficulties focused on the inelasticity of the money supply. If only the money supply could be made to respond adequately to the changing needs of business, it was argued, crises and panics would disappear.

The end result of the deliberations of the Monetary Commission and the ensuing debate, in which the banking community was actively engaged, was the Federal Reserve Act passed in December 1913. The act provided for a Board of Governors located in Washington and twelve regional Federal Reserve Banks to direct monetary affairs. National banks were required to become members of the system and other banks (chartered by individual states) were encouraged to do so. The issue of currency was concentrated in the hands of the Fed and provision was made for both currency and bank credit to expand and contract in response to the rhythms of the business world.

There are three main ways in which the Fed can act to provide the desired elasticity:

(1) *Reserve requirements.* Each member bank is required to set aside a part of the money deposited with it, either in cash or in the form of a deposit at the appropriate Federal Reserve

Bank, according to percentages established from time to time by the Board of Governors. Thus, if banks are mandated to keep 10 percent of their deposits in reserve, each member bank can then only invest or lend up to 90 percent of its deposits. By altering the reserve requirements, the Fed can reduce or expand the loan-making capacity of the member banks.

(2) *Loans to banks.* The Fed is empowered to lend to member banks against collateral consisting of part of the borrowing banks' assets (e.g., U.S. Treasury securities, municipal bonds, commercial and industrial loans). Interest is charged on these loans at what is called the rediscount rate, and the Fed tries to stimulate or discourage lending, as the case may be, by lowering or raising this rate. This activity (referred to in banking circles as taking place at "the discount window of the Fed") is obviously designed to influence the liquidity (or reserve position) of the member banks.

(3) *Open market operations.* When the Fed wants to increase the money supply, it buys Treasury securities in the open market (from banks, institutions, or individuals). These securities are paid for by checks drawn on the Federal Reserve. Since the checks will then be deposited in commercial banks, the latter will be provided with additional Federal Reserve money which counts as reserves on the basis of which they can expand their loans to customers (in the same way that borrowing at the discount window enhances the reserves of the member banks). When the Fed sells Treasury securities in the open market, the effect is the reverse. The buyers pay for their purchases with the checks on their banks which can then go into the Fed's account, depriving the members of reserves and hence reducing their power to lend. Through open market operations, in other words, the Fed causes money to move into or out of the banking system's reserves, expanding or contracting its capacity to lend.

In theory the flexibility thus gained was supposed to do away with depressions. Until the 1930s the conventional wisdom held that only accidents of nature (e.g., a series of bad harvests), war, or a faulty money supply could disturb the even tenor of business progress. Now that the United States had the Federal Reserve, depressions would be relegated to the historical past. So it was claimed until it became clear that all the power of all the central banks in all the advanced capitalist countries was unable to stave off the whirlwind of the Great Depression. That experience eventually brought economists either to accept or at least toy with the Keynesian diagnosis and prescriptions. Nevertheless, the old preconceptions hang on to this day, with Keynesians and non-Keynesians alike arguing whether it is this or that "mistake" by the Fed that is responsible for recurring economic contractions.

The underlying assumption of participants in these disputes is that fluctuations in the money supply govern economic conditions. In reality it is the other way around. The business cycle is not caused by money problems. Rather, the money problems are caused by the business cycle. The best the Fed can do is to smooth the path of the cycle by seeing to it that the banks have the wherewithal to meet what they perceive as their borrowers' legitimate needs, and rescuing banks in trouble to prevent financial panics. The Fed is more the follower than the leader of either the money supply or the business cycle. The point is that the main creators of money are the banks and not the Fed. And the amount of money the banks create depends on the demands of borrowers and their own competitive urge to grow and reap additional profits. But to understand this we need first to see how the banks create money.

### The Banks and the Money Supply

In popular usage money is equated with currency, that is, hard cash. In actuality, however, currency is only a minor component of the total money supply—less than 6 percent. The money that turns the wheels of commerce is located in checking and savings accounts, money market funds, and other financial depositories. The expansion and contraction of the money supply depends initially on the credit-creating activities of the banks. In other words, credit is the main source of money.

It should go without saying that the banks are in business to make profits. They do this by using the funds they receive as deposits either to buy interest-bearing securities (mainly U.S. government and municipal bonds) or to extend credit to customers. But they are restricted as to how much of their deposits they can use for these purposes since, as pointed out above, they are required by law to keep a percentage of their deposits in reserve. One would therefore imagine that if reserve requirements are, say, 20 percent, the banks could only invest or lend out 80 percent of their deposits. True, except that if we look at the banking system as a whole, a $1,000 deposit of cash can potentially grow to $5,000 or more of credit money. How this works is shown in Table 1, where we use two simplifying as-

*Table 1*

*How the Banks Create Money: An Illustration*

1. Assume an initial increase in deposits of $1,000.
2. Assume the Federal Reserve requires banks to keep a reserve of 20 percent against deposits.
3. Assume that the banks are always fully loaned out.

| *Bank* | *Increase in deposits (money supply)* — *1* — | *Increase in reserves (required)* — *2* — | *Increase in loans* — *3* — |
|---|---|---|---|
| Bank A | $1,000 | $200 | $800 |
| Bank B | 800 | 160 | 640 |
| Bank C | 640 | 128 | 512 |
| Bank D | 512 | 102 | 410 |
| Bank E | 410 | 82 | 328 |
| Bank F | 328 | 66 | 262 |

And so on until the following totals are reached:

| *All banks* | *Total increase in deposits (money supply)* | *Total increase in reserves (required)* | *Total increase in loans* |
|---|---|---|---|
| | $5,000 | $1,000 | $4,000 |

Illustration adapted from Howard J. Sherman, *Stagflation* (New York: Harper & Row, 1983), p. 181.

sumptions: (1) reserve requirements are 20 percent, and (2) all banks lend out the remaining 80 percent. Now let us follow the process of money expansion shown in the table.

We start with a $1,000 deposit of cash in Bank A made by, say, a shopkeeper. According to our assumptions, Bank A will put aside $200 in reserve and extend $800 of credit to another customer. That loan will be used to pay wages and buy materials if the borrower is a manufacturer, or to buy a house or a car, if the loan is to a consumer. Unless some of this distributed money ends up in a mattress, the $800 will eventually be deposited at one time or another in one or more banks. Suppose that all of the $800 lands as deposits in Bank B. (It doesn't matter for the point we are making whether the $800 is redeposited in Bank A or is spread out over a large number of other banks: we are merely simplifying a complex series of transactions.) Bank B now has an increase in its deposits of $800 (column 1), of which $160 is kept in reserve (column 2) and $640 (column 3) loaned out. The sequence continues as $512 ends up as an increase in Bank C's deposits. And so on. Eventually, the initial deposit grows to $5,000. (If the reserve requirement were assumed to be 10 percent, the final amount would be $10,000.)

### Limits to the Fed's Ability to Control

If this were the whole story, you might think it an easy matter for the Fed to keep credit expansion under tight control by using the tools provided to the Fed by the Federal Reserve Act and its subsequent modifications. But this is far from being the case, and the reason is that the financial world has invented or discovered many avenues for increasing the quantity of money and finding new ways to use the money supply that escape the Fed's grasp. The banks, it must always be kept in mind, are aggressive seekers of ever more profits. And the way they pursue this goal is by tirelessly expanding their business activity. For example, when deposits were not growing fast enough for the banks to be able to take advantage of the opportunities that arose in the late 1960s and 1970s, when inflation spiraled and the economy began to rely more and more on debt, they reached beyond their traditional role as recipients of deposits by themselves becoming major borrowers. The borrowed funds enabled them to lend still more money, contributing in the process to the ballooning of interest rates. Thus in 1980, the banks' borrowed funds amounted to almost 40 percent of their loans and investments, traditionally financed entirely by customers' deposits.

This development underscores a vital limitation on what the Fed can do to exercise *effective* control over the money supply. For what the banks achieved in boosting their business through borrowing is but one example of the ways in which the velocity of the circulation of money nullify the effectiveness of the Fed's actions. When the economy overheats during the upward phase of the cycle, the Fed may try to restrain what it sees as the unhealthy expansion of credit. How much it can do is to a large extent circumscribed by concern about endangering the stability of the banks. But even the moderate controls imposed are offset by an increase in velocity. Conversely, an attempt by the Fed to flood the money market in time of recession may be cancelled out by a decrease in the velocity of money.

Velocity—the intensity of use of money—has long been recognized as potentially decisive in determining the effectiveness of a given money supply. But velocity is an elusive factor which theorists have tried to ignore, with the result that they have misunderstood or gravely underestimated some of the most important developments of recent years. New and ingenious financial instruments have been introduced and nonbank financial intermediaries (investment trusts, insurance companies, money market funds, pension funds, etc.) have grown enormously in importance. Various forms of lending have developed whereby money is transferred back and forth from one institution to another, leading to a swelling of money flows over which the Fed has little power. What has been happening in this respect is indicated in Table 2. The first column gives the data for what has been traditionally considered to be the basic money supply, the one that the Fed was originally empowered to regulate. But this has paled in relative significance under the impact of the growth of new forms of borrowing and the increased role of all sorts of nonbank financial intermediaries. The total money supply, including the variety of forms that effective means of payment now assume, is given in the second column. As can be seen in column 3, the relative importance of "basic" money has been steadily declining from 45 percent in 1960 to 20 percent in 1983, which is another way of saying that new ways are constantly being sought and found to multi-

*Table 2*
*The Money Supply*

| | *Currency and all types of checking accounts** (1) | *The total money supply*** (2) | *Column (1) as a percent of column (2)* (3) |
|---|---|---|---|
| | — *Average daily figures in $ billions* — | | *Percent* |
| 1960 | $141.8 | $ 314.3 | 45.1% |
| 1965 | 169.5 | 480.3 | 35.3% |
| 1970 | 216.5 | 674.5 | 32.1% |
| 1975 | 291.1 | 1161.7 | 25.1% |
| 1980 | 414.1 | 1936.7 | 21.4% |
| 1983 | 521.1 | 2599.8 | 20.0% |

* This is the sum of currency, travelers' checks, and all checkable deposits (labeled by the Fed "M 1").

** This is the sum of column 1 plus savings and small-denomination time deposits at all depository institutions, overnight repurchase agreements (RPs) at commercial banks, overnight Eurodollars held by U.S. residents, money market mutual funds, large-denomination time deposits at all depository institutions, and term RPs at commercial banks and savings and loan associations (labeled by the Fed "M 3").

Source: *Economic Report of the President, 1984.*

ply the stock and speed up the velocity of money, whether to meet the needs of production and distribution or to swell the volume of transactions and hence the profits of financial enterprises.*

These developments have not gone unnoticed by the Fed. It has been seeking means to exercise some control over the new phenomena in the money market, but with little effect. The fundamental problem is that the economy has been increasingly dependent on debt creation, especially in the period of renewed stagnation since the 1960s. This has become so marked that many corporations now have to keep on borrowing just to service past debt—not unlike the situation in third world debtor countries. Too much interference with the debt structure could

---

* The spiraling tendency of money capital was pointed out over a hundred years ago by Marx: "With the development of the credit system and interest-bearing capital, all capital seems to double, or even treble, itself by the various modes in which the same capital, or perhaps the same claim on debt, appears in different forms in different hands." (*Capital*, Vol. 3.)

lead to serious and uncontrollable economic contraction. Even more: failure of the Fed to acquiesce in the worst excesses of the banks could precipitate a financial collapse. Under these circumstances the Fed can hardly do other than to follow the lead of the financial community. This point was clearly made by two financial specialists, a senior vice-president of Intercontinental Casualty Insurance Company and a vice-president of Chase Manhattan Bank, writing in the *Wall Street Journal:*

> The truth is that effective control of the money aggregates is achievable in theory, but not in practice. In theory the Fed could indeed inject or withdraw reserves from the banking system with no holds barred and an unswerving course. The problem is that this would produce much uncertainty over the availability of reserves. A misstep could lead to a wholesale calling in of loans and a spiralling descent to financial panic.
>
> That is why every week the Fed understandably acts in such a way as to fully accommodate the reserve requirements of the banking system (whatever they may be). The Fed can never refuse to provide the required reserves unless it would deliberately risk setting off a spiralling contraction of credit. So it contents itself with choosing between channels—open market operations or the Federal Reserve discount window—to supply the required reserves. (Eugene A. Birnbaum and Philip Braverman, "Monetarism—Broken Rudder of Reaganomics," *Wall Street Journal*, September 23, 1981)

It should be clear by now that a program for popular control of the Fed, such as advocated by some liberals and radicals, can be no panacea. Given the nature of capitalist enterprise and the system's financial superstructure, the Fed must, in the final analysis, be a servant rather than a master; and it will remain so no matter who manages it as long as the rest of the system remains unchanged. The Fed fulfills its function by resolving situations that might lead to financial panic (such as the rescue of Continental Illinois and helping stabilize the commercial paper market when Penn Central went bankrupt), and by helping to keep the banking system afloat despite its excesses.

There was a time when the Fed was able to play a more positive role. That was during the Second World War when it exercised its power to keep interest rates down to a bare minimum and in this and other ways helped to finance war expenditures. But that was also a time when the economy as a whole was influenced by other than immediate business (i.e., profit-making) interests. The government was then a major purchaser of goods and services, prices and wages were controlled, excess profits were taxed, and tight restrictions were imposed on credit creation.

Today, in sharp contrast, we have an economy burdened by speculation, waste, and unemployment—living to a large extent as a by-product of the financial community's debt creation. That being the case, it is illusory to imagine that better direction of the Fed can produce significant results. The money supply, whether in the form of currency or credit, has no magical properties. It is not money but profit-making and the operations of the market place that govern the course of the economy. What stands in the way of full employment, decent housing and adequate medical care, and an improved quality of life for all the people is not the absence of credit. Therefore, tinkering with the money supply or other traditional government mechanisms cannot produce what is needed. Rather, meaningful changes can only be achieved by reforms that challenge the ruling class's property and profit interests, with social goals taking precedence over private gain.

# *The Deficit, the Debt, and the Real World*

The latest fad in business journalism is to sound the alarm about the United States having become the biggest debtor in the world. This is intended to bring visions of our country sliding into a third world-type debt trap. But even those who don't draw such dire inferences nevertheless assume that a ballooning U.S. debt is in itself the prelude to economic disaster. That too is far from reality. In fact, both the size and the threatening nature of the debt burden are greatly exaggerated, largely the result of statistical mystification. Furthermore, to the extent that there is a debt problem, it is a symptom and not a cause of the real problems, including the potential of a financial breakdown, facing the United States and other capitalist nations.

What is important about the current spate of scare stories is that they feed into the prevailing ideology—the notion that the federal budget deficit and the accompanying debt burden are what is blocking a renewal of long-term growth, that all would be well in the economy if only the deficit could be eliminated. Never mind the persistence of mass unemployment, now officially close to 8 million but more realistically—according to estimates of the Council on International and Public Affairs—in excess of 15 million. Never mind the national epidemic of hunger, which according to the latest report of the Physician Task Force affects up to 20 million Americans. Never mind the absence of adequate health care for a large and growing sector of the population. All this needless human suffering in the world's richest country pales into insignificance compared to a swelling national debt fed by an ever-increasing deficit.

A closer look at the relevant facts immediately reveals that

This article originally appeared in the May 1985 issue of *Monthly Review*.

the size of the debt in and of itself is far from being the clear and present danger we are being warned against. It is of course true that the outstanding national debt has been piling up at a very rapid rate in recent years, increasing almost 80 percent during Reagan's first term (see Table 1, column 1). But that

*Table 1*
*The Public Debt and the Gross National Product*

| *Year* | *Federal debt outstanding at end of year** (in billions of dollars) | *Gross National Product* (in billions of dollars) | *Debt as a percent of Gross National Product (percent)* |
|---|---|---|---|
| 1940 | 45.0 | 100.0 | 45.0 |
| 1945 | 278.1 | 212.4 | 130.9 |
| 1960 | 290.2 | 506.5 | 57.3 |
| 1970 | 369.0 | 992.7 | 37.2 |
| 1980 | 930.2 | 2,631.7 | 35.0 |
| 1984 | 1,663.0 | 3,664.2 | 45.4 |

* Calendar years prior to 1970 and fiscal years for 1970 and later.
*Sources: President's Economic Report,* 1969 and 1985.

is only one part of the picture: we must also consider the magnitude of the debt in relation to the economy as a whole. Clearly, the greater total output and income the better an economy can cope with a given amount of debt. In the third column of Table 1 we see the outstanding debt as a percent of the Gross National Product for selected years between 1940 and 1984. Viewed in historical perspective, it is apparent that current debt levels are not abnormal. Today's national debt as a percent of GNP is about the same as that of 1940 and considerably below 1960. The most striking comparison of all is with the debt load produced by the Second World War. At the end of 1945, the ratio of debt to GNP was more than 130 percent, almost three times larger than the current figure.

What these comparisons indicate is that a large debt need not hold back economic growth or bring disastrous results. This is not necessarily a universal economic truth, since the ability to cope with debt varies from one country and period to another. Here we are merely focusing on the United States with its enormous productive capacity and rich natural resources. What appears at first sight to have been an overwhelmingly huge postwar debt was no obstacle to this country's growth. In fact the contrary was the case. The debt had been built up under conditions that created a backlog of effective demand, which together with successful postwar labor struggles for higher wages gave a substantial initial boost to a new era of growth. In addition, a number of other favorable factors were at work at that time to stimulate a long wave of prosperity, punctuated only by a series of relatively mild recessions. The federal debt was increased from time to time, either to overcome recessions or to finance wars. But it grew at a much slower pace than the expanding economy as a whole, with a resulting sharp decline in its relative size.

What is new today is not the acceleration of debt accumulation but its occurrence in a period of deepening stagnation. When the prosperity-supporting postwar stimuli began to peter out, the economy was forced to rely more and more heavily on increasing debt, both private and public. A growing national debt thus became a crucial instrument in the struggle to keep the economy afloat. And under these changed conditions, the debt grew faster than the economy. The debt-producing deficit was no longer a mere counter-cyclical tool, it became an essential prop in the upward phase of the cycle as well. That is why, as shown in Table 1, the relative size of the debt turned dramatically upward after 1980. What needs to be stressed is thus neither the magnitude of the debt nor the reversal of the trend. Seen in their proper context, indeed, these are essentially the symptoms of an underlying faltering economy. It follows that the focus of today's debate is totally misdirected. All eyes are on the size of the deficit and not on what makes it necessary.

Nor is proper attention being paid to the uses to which the deficit is put and the way it is financed. It would be one thing if the deficit were being devoted to lightening the impact of stagnation on the poor, the aged, and the unemployed. It is something entirely different when, as at present, the deficit brings about a waste of resources and an unconscionable investment in armaments that can lead to the destruction of life on this planet.

Equally absent from the debate is the method of financing the deficit. Since it is wholly covered by the issuance of Treasury securities, each year's deficit adds to the outstanding debt and the budget's interest burden. When high interest rates are combined with continuous large deficits, that burden is bound to grow very rapidly and to become an ever larger part of the budget. Already in 1984 interest on the accumulated debt accounted for almost two-thirds of that year's deficit! What this means is that instead of being used for socially useful purposes, a growing portion of the deficit is siphoned off to fill the coffers of wealthy bondholders.

The conventional wisdom maintains that it cannot be otherwise. That is based first on the belief that there is no sensible way of financing the deficit other than by borrowing—a fallacy we will discuss below. Second, it is taken for granted that interest rates must remain high as long as the deficit is so large. Implicit here is the assumption that the private credit markets are sacrosanct, even though a large part of the credit generated each year is used for purely financial skulduggery in the mad rush to buy and sell corporations and to feed wild speculation. Given the truism that the level of interest rates is determined by the relation between the supply and the demand for credit, and assuming that any interference with the private credit market is taboo, it follows that the main cause of high interest rates is government demand for credit. Reasoning of this type not only lacks logic, it also ignores an important lesson of past experience, as was pointed out above (p. 110):

> But are the high interest rates that impose such a heavy burden on the budget inevitable? What happened during the Second World War proves beyond a shadow of doubt that they are not. In the war years from 1942 to 1945, the average annual deficit was 23 percent of the Gross National Product, and of course that was at a time when available economic resources were stretched to the limit. Yet the interest rate on three-month Treasury bills in those years was less than one-half of 1 percent, and on highest-grade corporate bonds it was less than 3 percent. Thus far in the 1980s, in contrast, the average annual deficit has been only 3.8 percent of GNP, and there has been plenty of slack in the economy (at least 10 million unemployed and a quarter of manufacturing capacity idle). Yet the average interest rate has been over 11 percent on three-month Treasury bills and 13 percent on AAA corporation bonds.

The explanation for this striking difference is not hard to find. The clearcut overriding priority in the early 1940s was winning the war. On the civilian front this called for a coordinated production effort, a firm grip on the economy, and the rallying of popular support. To that end the administration, still under the influence of the New Deal approach to social problems, undertook to minimize the cost of financing the war, to prevent inflation, and to protect the people's living standards. A number of related policies were adopted to achieve these aims: wage, price, and profit controls; rationing of scarce consumer goods; restrictions on credit; imposition of a lid on interest rates; etc. While all was not perfect in either the policies or their execution, still the wartime experience proved that it is possible to manage a huge deficit while maintaining low interest rates and without undue sacrifice of the welfare of the people.

With the war safely won, U.S. policies quickly adapted to the new situation. Ever since colonial days the American bourgeoisie had seen itself as destined to rule over a worldwide empire.* Now at least the long-sought prize seemed within easy reach. With a war-weary world in a condition bordering on chaos and the U.S. economy at the peak of its strength, a full-blown program of global dominance was not long in taking shape. The domestic political coalition that had sustained the New Deal was soon converted to support the country's revitalized imperialism. A prosperous economy made possible concessions to the working class whose leaders were in any case far from hostile to ruling-class ambitions. In the absence of significant political opposition, the only effective constraints on U.S. capitalism were those that arose from its own inner contradictions.

Beneath the surface these contradictions gradually ripened, eventually sapping the foundations of prosperity, producing increasingly severe recessions, and in reaction generating a pathological and increasingly fragile financial superstructure. In this hot-house climate the controls that had been imposed in the 1930s to prevent a possible repeat of 1929 were relaxed or

* The classic study in this connection is R.W. Van Alstyne, *The Rising American Empire* (New York: Quadrangle, 1960), which should be studied by everyone seriously interested in American history.

abandoned. Neither sensible restraint nor the needs of the people were permitted to stand in the way of unleashing the potentially explosive money markets. For the financial community, with its uniquely narrow focus on the main chance and the bottom line, these new policies opened up a new world of opportunity. Interest rate ceilings were lifted, restraints on the expansion of banks relaxed, corporate taxes sharply cut, and new modes of speculation added to the old. It was this financial explosion, not the federal deficit, that pushed interest rates into the stratosphere.

In this climate of frenzied finance—so reminiscent of earlier episodes in the history of capitalism going back to the South Sea Bubble of the early eighteenth century—the lessons of the New Deal and the war years are conveniently ignored. The economy as currently structured is sacrosanct. All blame for present troubles and future dangers is then heaped on the deficit and the federal debt load: these are proclaimed to be the source of all evil. And this in turn becomes an ideological trap for liberals and radicals as well as conservatives. Since the real causes of the economy's failures are unknown or ignored, the focus of debate shifts to how best to restrain the deficit. The litany is a familiar one: jobs are lost because a strong dollar cuts exports and stimulates imports; the dollar is strong because interest rates are too high; the cause of high interest rates is the large deficit. And since it is supposedly imperative that the deficit be reduced, the agenda shifts to debate over where and how to cut welfare programs which—so the argument goes—we can no longer afford.

All right, some may say, we agree that the deficit issue is a mystification that deflects attention from the real issues. But what about the enormous debt? Isn't there a danger that a debt of this magnitude that keeps on growing will eventually lead to national bankruptcy? If the government has to keep on borrowing just to service the debt, what will happen if there aren't enough buyers willing to absorb the debt instruments? Answers to such questions cannot be reasonably given for all countries and for all times. But *as for the United States at this time,* the answers are not that difficult; and as we examine the evidence, we will be able to see that these questions are not relevant with respect to the foreseeable future either. We do not mean to imply that there are no potential questions associated with the management of the debt, nor are we glossing over possible financial turmoil that may be associated with the debt. The point we wish to make is that national bankruptcy is simply not an issue.

An examination of the data presented in Table 2 will help to explain that statement. It shows the Fed's estimates of the distribution of the debt among different categories of owners of Treasury securities. The information is as of the end of June 1984, the latest date for which complete estimates are now available.

The first thing to notice is that a large portion of the debt is owned not by the public but by government entities. The U.S. government invests its reserves for social security, medicare, federal pensions, and other so-called trust funds in U.S. Treasury certificates. These holdings amount to 17 percent of the outstanding debt. In addition, the Federal Reserve banks own about 10 percent of the debt. This amount expands and contracts from time to time, since these debt instruments are used by the Fed in its attempt to regulate the money supply. About 11 percent of the debt is held by state and local governments. Although the states and localities are formally independent, their finances are intricately tied in with the fiscal operations of the federal government. Adding up these holdings, we find that 38 percent of the public debt is owed to government institutions.

Clearly, bankruptcy is a meaningless concept when applied to the debt held by public bodies. Nor does it necessarily apply to the additional 27 percent owned by the banks. In the worst scenario, or even long before that, nationalization of the banks could quickly reduce the pressure arising from the needs to renew or service the debt. If we add the holdings of the banks to those of government bodies, we reach a total of 65 percent of the debt that could, if necessary, be handled as an internal government matter.

The 11 percent owed to foreigners is also of little significance in view of the role of the U.S. dollar as an international currency. Foreigners can be paid off, if need be, by sending

*Table 2*
*Holders of the U.S. Government Debt,*
*June 30, 1984*

| *Owners of U.S. government securities* | *Amount in $ billions* | | *Percent of total* | |
|---|---|---|---|---|
| *Government bodies* | *573.5* | | *38.0%* | |
| U.S. government agencies and trust funds | | 257.6 | | 17.0 |
| Federal reserve banks | | 152.9 | | 10.1 |
| State and local governments | | 165.0 | | 10.9 |
| *Banks* | *414.1* | | *27.4* | |
| Commercial banks | | 182.3 | | 12.1 |
| Savings banks | | 231.8 | | 15.3 |
| *Foreigners* | *171.5* | | *11.3* | |
| *All others* | *351.6* | | *23.3* | |
| Companies | | 106.9 | | 7.1 |
| Individuals: Savings bonds | | 72.9 | | 4.8 |
| Other treasuries | | 69.3 | | 4.6 |
| Miscellaneous* | | 102.5 | | 6.8 |
| *Total debt* | *1,512.7* | | *100.0* | |

* Includes money market funds, corporate pension trust funds, nonprofit institutions, dealers and brokers, certain U.S. deposit accounts, and government-sponsored agencies.

*Sources:* *Federal Reserve Bulletin,* April 1985, except for the data on savings banks which were derived from Board of Governors of the Federal Reserve System, *Flow of Funds Accounts, Assets and Liabilities Outstanding, 1960-83* and *Flow of Funds Accounts,* Fourth Quarter 1984.

them U.S. dollars, just as long as the central bankers of other countries continue to use dollars as a major part of their foreign reserves.

What is left then is the 23 percent held by corporations and individuals. The $340 billion involved here, however, is a relatively minor matter in comparison with the size of the U.S. economy—less than 10 percent of GNP.

The discussion thus far has been based on the tacit assumption that the only feasible way to finance deficits and service the debt is by borrowing. There is however an alternative—the issuance of currency on which no interest is paid and which would therefore eliminate the need for ever larger budgets to service the debt. We are now entering upon a most sensitive area, one that has long been off-limits to respectable folk. That printing currency to cover a deficit inevitably produces uncontrollable inflation has become an article of unquestioned faith. There is of course considerable historical evidence of runaway inflation created by reckless use of the printing presses. But it does not follow that it must aways be so.

The cause of past hyper-inflations has never been the printing of currency. Rather, such inflations are due to the issue of too much currency in relation to the capacity of an economy to produce goods and services to satisfy effective demand. Thus, a country that finances a war by printing money and cannot, because of the war, produce enough consumer goods to absorb the resulting flood of currency opens the door to hyper-inflation. Similarly, an irresponsible government that prints money without regard to the inflationary danger is asking for trouble. But that is not necessarily the case for a country that has a surplus of food, idle productive capacity, and mass unemployment—as is and has for a long time been the situation in the United States. Of course this financial method contains dangers and must be handled with caution. For example, paying off the accumulated debt in one fell swoop might very well create monetary disturbances and initiate a dangerous inflationary trend. But what if the annual deficit, or part of it, were financed by issuing new currency? Under existing conditions this is a method which, if carefully handled and accompanied by appropriate controls on the creation of credit by the private economy, could be usefully introduced into the government's management of the deficit and the debt.

In raising this issue, we are not offering a cure. Rather, the purpose is to open up a subject that has, in a sense, been hypocritically closed. The accepted doctrine that borrowing is the *only* way to finance the deficit brooks no questioning. Yet the same kind of objection to considering the currency-issuance road can be equally applied to current practices. The supposed advantages of the borrowing approach are based on a number of dubious assumptions: there is assumed to be a fixed supply of savings available for investment; when the government borrows a portion of this stock of savings, the amount available for private investment is supposedly reduced; hence there is no inflationary effect. But the notion that there is a fixed supply of savings ignores the extent to which credit can be expanded (see "Money Out of Control," MR, December 1984). Moreover, the securities issued by the Treasury are widely used for precisely this kind of credit expansion.

In earlier days, the Treasury financed the national debt by selling primarily long-term bonds (with maturities of ten years or more). During New Deal days and the Second World War period, between 55 and 80 percent of Treasury securities were long-term bonds. Bonds of this duration could fit in with some of the assumptions mentioned above, since they represent in large measure socked-away money that would not reappear in the money market for a long time.

But all that has changed in the go-go speculative era that since the 1960s has flourished alongside the explosion of private debt. Now, long-term Treasuries account for less than 14 percent of the debt. The dominant debt instruments these days are short-term: currently about 75 percent have less than a five-year maturity, while 43 percent are less than one year (a large portion of these are for only three or six months). These are traded and retraded in rapid succession and have become almost a substitute for money in certain financial transactions. They are above all used as a medium of credit expansion. One way this works is by the use of so-called repos (repurchase agreements). For example, when a bank needs funds to back up the granting of additional credit, it sells its own Treasuries with a promise to repurchase them at an agreed price and on an agreed date. This is in effect a way to borrow at a lower rate of interest than the acquired money is expected to earn. Not only the banks but brokers, security dealers, and other operators in the money market use the same device. In addition firms and businessmen buy short-term Treasuries with idle cash and resell them at short notice. Then there are the traders and speculators who buy and sell Treasuries as a business, carried on with borrowed money. How extensive the resulting trade and speculation in Treasury securities has become was highlighted in a recent *New York Times* editorial: "More than $200 billion worth of Government securities are traded in a normal day—a hundred times more money than changes hands on the New York Stock Exchange." (April 12, 1985) This may be an overstatement, but probably not a serious one.

We are of course aware that we have been raising a lot of questions without attempting to provide definitive answers. Our purpose is to try to shock people out of an all-too-easy acceptance of stock stereotypes that are imposed on us every day of our lives by the media and the certified establishment authorities. The deficit and the national debt are, after all, bookkeeping entries. We live in a real world of human beings a few of whom are rich and most of whom are either poor or barely making it. We ought not to allow ourselves to get these two realms mixed up. We shouldn't be deterred from struggling to solve the real problems of the real world by the mystifications and obfuscations of those who run the show and whose main objective in life is to keep it that way.

# *The Financial Explosion*

Credit where credit is due. For a long time now we have been harping in this space on the theme of a monetary system out of control; of the wild proliferation of new financial institutions, instruments, and markets; of the unchecked spread of a speculative fever certainly more pervasive and perhaps even more virulent than any recorded in the long history of capitalism's get-rich-quick obsessions. With few exceptions, accredited economists, as is their wont, have ignored these bizarre goings-on: they are not part of the way the economy is supposed to operate and are hence unworthy of "scientific" attention. The media, on the other hand, especially the serious business press, have reported the facts as they have unfolded—the rapid growth of options and futures markets, the near bankruptcy and rescue by the government of one of the country's largest banks, etc., etc.—but have generally steered clear of any attempt to put these discrete developments into a coherent account of an enormously powerful dynamic process rooted in the nature of the economic system and loaded with implications for the country's future.

Now, very much to its credit, *Business Week* has broken ranks and made a serious attempt to fill the gap. The result, a cover story entitled "The Casino Society" in its issue of September 16, is a noteworthy journalistic achievement. Colorfully written and packed with facts, it tells an exciting story well worth the careful attention of everyone interested in understanding the current economic scene.

What is the casino society? Here, in an introduction (in-

This article originally appeared in the December 1985 issue of *Monthly Review.*

cluded on the cover of the magazine) is *Business Week's* shorthand answer:

> No, it's not Las Vegas or Atlantic City. It's the U.S. financial system. The volume of transactions has boomed far beyond anything needed to support the economy. Borrowing—politely called leverage—is getting out of hand. And futures enable people to play the market without owning a share of stock. The result: the system is tilting from investment to speculation.

Data in support of these statements are focused on the expansion in the volume of financial transactions. A composite quotation can serve as a summary:

> On the NYSE [New York Stock Exchange], 108 million shares change hands daily, up from 49 million five years ago. In the government securities market, trading volume is averaging $76 billion a day, quadrupling 1980's level. Yet this growth seems tame compared with the action in financial futures and options trading pits. For example, daily volume in Treasury-bond and T-bill futures tripled in 1984 alone, to $26 billion.... The volume of financial transactions in this country has soared beyond calculation—and beyond economic purpose.... Stocks are not greatly overpriced, and margin borrowing is modest [in contrast to 1929]. But the speculative use of debt and other forms of leverage is pandemic in the rest of the financial world. "The markets," says NYSE Chairman John J. Phelan, "are leveraged to the teeth." Washington, of course, is setting an unrivalled standard of profligacy, running a $180-billion annual budget deficit. Total federal debt doubled during the 1970s and hit $1 trillion in 1981, the Reagan administration's first year. Next year, it will top $2 trillion. Meanwhile, borrowing is surging all across the economy. Total debt of households, corporations, and governments jumped by a postwar record of 14 percent, to $7.1 trillion, in 1984. That's considerably faster than the economy is growing. Credit-market debt now stands at an ominous 1.95 times GNP, compared with 1.68 a decade ago. [Moreover, there is a vast debt equivalent which doesn't show on anyone's books.] Barred by law from underwriting mutual funds or commercial paper, the big banks have been retaliating against Wall Street's incursions by offering corporate clients liquidity in the form of commitments—to make loans, to buy or sell foreign currency, or to guarantee the obligations of a creditor. Banks can charge tidy fees for making these commitments and yet not set aside capital to back them up, as they would loans. At the end of 1984 these "off-balance-sheet liabilities" at the 15 largest banks totaled $930 billion, or about 8 percent more than their assets.

Here, then, are the kind of figures which, taken together, give an idea of the fantastic dimensions of the financial explosion that has taken place in the United States in the last decade or so.*

On the question of what it all means—i.e., of the relation of the financial explosion to the performance of the economy as a whole—the *Business Week* story has little to contribute beyond dark hints and ominous warnings of unknown perils that lie ahead. But the editors of the magazine, in an accompanying editorial, show that they are fully aware of the problem, and their way of formulating it has the merit of pointing toward the kind of analysis that is needed: "Although the emergence of the casino society," they write, "coincided with the economy's prolonged slowdown in the mid-1970s, nobody can demonstrate which is the chicken and which the egg. But clearly, slow growth and today's rampant speculative binge are locked in some kind of symbiotic embrace." What we need to know is the nature of this embrace.

It is necessary to rule out at the outset a frequently encountered notion that what we are now witnessing is simply the most recent of a long series of speculative manias that have punctuated the history of capitalism since at least the famous "South Sea Bubble" of 1720. Beginning as long ago as the 1820s, speculative excesses of this kind became a normal feature of the capitalist business cycle, getting under way in the later stages of the boom and foreshadowing the panic and collapse to come. It was, in fact, the regular recurrence of this pattern in the United States that, after the panic of 1907, led to the establishment of the Federal Reserve System. The present situation, however, is very far from being an end-of-the-boom phenomenon. Its origins can plausibly be dated even earlier than the mid-1970s, and it has been more or less steadily building up ever since. This being also the period when economic stagnation set in after the long postwar upswing of the 1950s and 1960s, we

* The whole phenomenon can be approached from a wider angle, focusing not only on the volume of financial transactions but also on the rapid expansion—relative as well as absolute—of the financial sector of the economy in terms of real resources (employment and capital investment). See "Production and Finance" in this volume, pp. 93-105, where some rough estimates of this kind are attempted.

evidently need to identify a causal mechanism different from the one that characterized the prewar business cycle.

The problem in our view, can be divided into two parts. First, why did the stagnation that had dominated the economy in the 1930s return in the 1970s? And, second, why, in the conditions of the 1970s, did a stagnant economy become a breeding ground for a financial explosion?

These are of course questions that in one form or another have been dealt with many times in these pages. Here we will only touch on the main points that need to be kept in mind.

First—and in a sense the real crux of the whole matter—in a mature monopoly capitalist society there is always a strong tendency to stagnation. In some historical contexts this tendency takes over and dominates the economic scene, while in others it is held at bay and the economy experiences a long wave of expansion punctuated only by brief and mild recessions. The period beginning at the end of the Second World War was an example par excellence of the latter kind. Why was this so?*

The answer is that the war altered the givens of the world economic situation in ways that vastly expanded the scope of profitable investment opportunities. The main factors were as follows: (1) the pressing need to make good wartime damage; (2) the existence of an enormous potential demand for goods and services the production of which had been eliminated or greatly reduced during the war (houses, automobiles, appliances, etc.); (3) a huge pool of purchasing power accumulated during the war by firms and individuals which could be used to transform potential into effective demand; (4) the establishment of U.S. global hegemony as a result of the war: the U.S. dollar became the basis of the international monetary system, prewar trade and currency blocs were dismantled, and the conditions for relatively free capital movements were created—all of which served to fuel an enormous expansion of international trade; (5) civilian spinoffs from military technology, especially electronics and jet planes; and (6) the build-up by the United States of a huge permanent armaments industry, spurred on by

* What follows is taken, with minor modifications, from "Why Stagnation?" this volume, pp. 29-38.

major regional wars in Korea and Indochina. Very important but too often overlooked is the fact that these developments were in due course reflected in a fundamental change in the business climate. The pessimism and caution left over from the 1930s was not dissipated immediately, but when it became clear that the postwar boom had much deeper roots than merely repairing the damages and losses of the war itself, the mood changed into one of long-run optimism. A great investment boom in all the essential industries of a modern capitalist society was triggered: steel, autos, energy, ship-building, chemicals, and many more. Capacity was rapidly built up in the leading capitalist countries and in a few of the more advanced nations of the third world like Mexico, Brazil, India, and South Korea.

In seeking the causes of the reemergence of stagnation in the 1970s, the crucial point to keep in mind is that every one of the forces that powered the long postwar expansion was, and was bound to be, self-limiting. This is indeed part of the very nature of investment: it not only responds to a demand, it also satisfies the demand. Wartime damage was repaired. Demand deferred during the war was satisfied. The process of building up new industries (including a peacetime arms industry) requires a lot more investment than maintaining them. Expanding industrial capacity always ends up by creating *over*capacity: a strong incentive to invest generates a burst of investment which in turn undermines the incentive to invest. This is the secret of the long postwar boom and of the return of stagnation in the 1970s.

We turn now to the second part of the problem at issue: why, in the conditions of the 1970s, did a stagnant economy become the breeding ground for a financial explosion?

The answer here is more complicated than the answer to the return-to-stagnation question, but its main elements—even if not their specific form of interaction or ranking in order of importance—are clear enough. To begin with, the financial sector of the economy which had been moribund in the 1930s and under tight control throughout the war experienced a vigorous growth during the next three decades. Between 1945 and 1975, while the GNP grew by a factor of 7.3 (reflecting price inflation as well as real growth), the debt of nonfinancial business firms and consumers increased 19 times, with the bellwether interest rate on 3-month treasury bills rising from 0.375 percent to 5.8 percent. Up to about 1960, this expansion of the financial sector was pretty much in step with, and basically resulted from, the long postwar upswing in the underlying economy. After that, especially under the stimulus of the Vietnam war, the financial sector began to grow more rapidly than the economy as a whole. Already in 1975 we wrote in this space, "The specter haunting today's capitalist world is the possible collapse of its financial institutions and an associated world economic crisis." ("Banks: Skating on Thin Ice," February 1975) Against this background, what should we expect the consequences to be of the relapse into stagnation signalled by the severe recession of 1973-75?

In this connection we must remember that banks and other financial businesses, being capitalist institutions, operate under the same growth imperatives as do industrial corporations. They are spurred on by competition and the drive to expand the profit base. Since the commodity they deal in is money, the key to growth and higher profit lies in marketing an ever larger volume of debt. And if one source of demand for financing falters, they naturally work all the harder to cultivate others. So it was that with the slowdown of industrial investment as the long postwar wave subsided, the financial sector intensified the hunt which has continued to this day for alternative customers. It was no accident that it was just about at this time that U.S. banks started shovelling out funds abroad, especially to third world countries, many of which, as we now know, were seduced into taking on vastly more debt than they would ever be able to service, let alone repay.

But the money-pushers were busy at home as well as abroad, and it wasn't long before the debt-creation process took on the character of a self-contained operation, with financial institutions (and wealthy individuals) playing leading roles on both sides of the market, i.e., as both suppliers and demanders. How this works is perhaps best illustrated by the rapid growth of money-market funds, which got their start by offering higher interest rates than banks, with a resulting flood of money from the banks to the funds. The banks then raised their rates to get deposits back. Billions of dollars worth of back-and-forth financial transactions thus pushed up interest rates without any relation to the underlying production and circulation of useful goods and services. Other examples of the proliferation of purely financial transactions are legion: most of the multi-billion-dollar activity in the area of corporate mergers and acquisitions is of this type, as indeed is the great bulk of speculative trading in markets specialized to an ever widening spectrum of negotiable assets: commodities, foreign exchange, stocks and bonds, futures and options (even options on futures!), and so on and on. The crucial point, and one that is almost totally missing from traditional economic discourse, is that the financial sphere has the potential to become an autonomous subsystem of the economy as a whole, with an enormous capacity for self-expansion.

Once the expansion process gets fully under way, as it was bound to do in the context of the reappearance of stagnation in the 1970s, it tends to feed on itself: like a cancer, it lacks internal control mechanisms. The only way it can be brought under control is through external intervention. In the case of cancer this may take the form of surgery or radiation or drugs; in the case of the financial system the only possibility is government intervention. But with the economy slowing down, governments, far from being interested in putting on the financial brakes, or even looking to the condition of the braking system with a view to future use, were concerned to facilitate financial expansion in the belief that this was one way, and perhaps the most effective way, of countering stagnation.

Thus federal deficits, reflecting the government's generally expansionist policies, practically tripled, from an annual average of $13.6 billion in 1970-74 to $39.4 billion in the next five years (and again to $116.6 billion in 1980-84!). And whenever the debt expansion process showed signs of stalling, either because of restrictive laws and regulations dating back to the days of the New Deal and the Second World War or because of a threatened failure of a big bank or corporation that could trigger a chain reaction of bankruptcies, the authorities came to the rescue by reinterpreting the laws and relaxing the regulations and/or by emergency injection of money by the Federal Reserve to endangered banks or by government subsidies, loans, or loan guarantees to ailing firms or industries. These actions in turn broadened the base for a renewed expansion of debt and greater dependence of the economy as a whole on the ballooning of credit.

•

If the foregoing analysis is accepted, certain conclusions follow.

First, the financial explosion has in fact been a force counteracting stagnation. Not of course that it has done away with stagnation but in the more limited sense that without it stagnation would have been worse. There are two reasons for this: (1) The expansion of the financial sector has opened up significant opportunities for profitable investment in office buildings, transportation and communications equipment, business machines, etc.* (2) The sharp increase in interest income associated with the financial explosion—net interest rose from 6.5 percent of national income in 1974 to 9.6 percent in 1984—plus the enormous profits raked in by Wall Street and its lesser counterparts around the country have acted as an important stimulus to consumption, especially in the booming area of luxury goods and services. Without these props to both investment and consumption, the performance of the economy these past few years would certainly have been much worse than it actually was.

Let us pause to ponder the meaning of these facts. Conventional wisdom has it that financial excesses of the kind we have been discussing that recur every so often in capitalist societies are deplorable aberrations that corrupt people, waste resources, and disrupt the normal functioning of the economy. As the *Business Week* editorial on the casino society puts it: "The case can be made that the casino society channels far too much talent and energy into financial shell games rather than into producing real goods and services, and that it is a significant drag on eco-

* As shown in "The Strange Recovery of 1983-1984," this volume, pp. 68-78, these are precisely the areas of buoyant capital formation in the economic recovery of the early 1980s.

nomic growth." On analysis, however, this turns out to be a much more complicated statement than may appear at first sight.

Does the casino society in fact channel far too much talent and energy into financial shell games? Yes, of course. No sensible person could deny it. Does it do so at the expense of producing real goods and services? Absolutely not. There is no reason whatever to assume that if you could deflate the financial structure, the talent and energy now employed there would move into productive pursuits. They would simply become unemployed and add to the country's already huge reservoir of idle human and material resources. Is the casino society a significant drag on economic growth? Again, absolutely not. What growth the economy has experienced in recent years, apart from that attributable to an unprecedented peacetime military build-up, has been almost entirely due to the financial explosion.

We can now see why, though everyone deplores the increasingly outrageous excesses of the financial explosion and is aware of its inherent dangers, nothing is being done—or even seriously proposed—to bring it under control. Quite the contrary: every time a catastrophe threatens, the authorities spring into action to put out the fire—and in the process spread more inflammable material around for the next flare-up to feed on. The reason is simply that if the explosion were brought under control, even assuming that it could be done without triggering a chain reaction of bankruptcies, the overall economy would be sent into a tailspin. The metaphor of the man with a tiger by the tail fits the case to a tee.

Where is it all leading? Or perhaps the question should be reformulated: What alternative scenarios make sense as we try to peer into what is at best a very murky future?

First, a bust of classic dimensions. This indeed has been a plausible outcome for a long time, and there have been at least half a dozen occasions since the recession of 1973-75 when it seemed on the verge of happening. The remarkable thing about this scenario, however, is not that it could happen but that it hasn't. And the reason of course is that the government has always successfully intervened to keep it from happening. We have now reached a situation in which (in the words of *Business Week*) "the financial system is more dependent than ever on swift intervention by government authorities to forestall disaster."

Continued successful intervention cannot be taken for granted but neither can it be ruled out. And this suggests a plausible alternative scenario that ought to be given serious attention. What would be the long-run implications of government's undertaking to guarantee the financial system against the kind of collapse and generalized deflation that was the prelude to the Great Depression of the 1930s?

We don't know the answer, nor do we know of any attempt by others to provide one. Perhaps even raising the question in this form at the present stage is premature: more experience may be needed before the elements of an answer can begin to fall into place. But discussion is certainly in order, and we would be glad to hear the ideas of any readers who are convinced, as we are, that sooner or later—and perhaps sooner rather than later—the left in this country is going to be forced by events to define a position on this and related questions.

# III

# *The United States and the Global Economy*

# *The Regime of Capital*

During the last half century the influence of Marxism on the social sciences, as understood and taught in the advanced capitalist countries, has steadily increased. This has happened in two ways—through younger social scientists becoming converted to Marxist ways of thinking and acquiring positions in academia; and through bourgeois social scientists being exposed to Marxist work in these fields and frequently finding aspects of it valuable, or at least worthy of study. History has probably been the discipline most affected. It is hardly an exaggeration to say that most serious work in history nowadays takes for granted the validity of some of the basic tenets of historical materialism—without of course necessarily coming to characteristically Marxist conclusions. Sociology and anthropology have also been much influenced, often in subtle and even unconscious ways. Political science—or, as it is sometimes more appropriately called, "government" or "politics"—has been less affected, and economics least of all.

This is not to deny the reality of the Marxist revolt against mainstream orthodoxy in economics: quite possibly there are proportionally more younger Marxists in economics than in any of the other social sciences. If so, however, this may well be a consequence of the consistent refusal on the part of the leading lights of the profession to take Marxism seriously, let alone allow it to influence their thinking. The more rigid the orthodoxy, the more extreme the reaction against it.

Of course there have always been exceptions. Joseph Schumpeter not only took Marx seriously; he paid him the com-

This article, by Paul M. Sweezy, originally appeared in the January 1986 issue of *Monthly Review*.

pliment of emulation, Schumpeter's overall vision of capitalism being consciously designed as an alternative to Marx's. And Keynes, despite occasional disparaging remarks about Marx in his published writings was in important respects closer to Marx's way of thinking about money and capital accumulation than he was to the accepted neoclassical orthodoxy.* But Keynes's followers—again with exceptions, most notably Joan Robinson—moved away from rather than toward further reconciliation with Marxist ideas. Curiously, their effort on the whole was to minimize what Keynes rightly believed to have been his own break with neoclassical theory: bastard Keynesianism, to use Joan Robinson's pithy description, was in reality an ignominious re-

* It has only become known since Keynes's death, through the publication of his *Collected Works*, that he explicitly recognized this affinity to Marx. I quote from a very interesting article by Dudley Dillard ("Marx and Keynes: A Centennial Appraisal," written for a symposium commemorating the hundredth anniversary of Marx's death and Keynes's birth, published in the *Journal of Post Keynesian Economics*, Spring 1984): "One of the rare occasions in which Keynes praised Marx occurred in a 1933 draft of the *General Theory* when it was still called "The Monetary Theory of Employment." Keynes credits Marx with the "pregnant observation . . . that the nature of production in the actual world is not, as economists seem often to suppose, a case of C-M-C′, i.e., of exchanging commodities (or effort) for money in order to obtain another commodity (or effort). That may be the standpoint of private consumers, but it is not the attitude of *business*, which is a case of M-C-M′, ie., a parting with money for commodities (or effort) in order to obtain more money." (The quotation from Keynes comes from his *Collected Works*, Vol. 29, p. 81.)

When Keynes's use of the Marxian formulas C-M-C and M-C-M′ was first called to my attention (by an article by Roy Rotheim, "Keynes' Monetary Theory of Value," *Journal of Post Keynesian Economics*, Smmer 1981), I wrote to Joan Robinson (March 2, 1982): "I was fascinated to learn from an article by Roy J. Rotheim . . . that Keynes was influenced by Marx's C-M-C and M-C-M′ schemas. From his published remarks about Marx—consigning him to the underworld of Gesell and Major Douglas, etc.—I had no idea of this link. Could he have picked up Marx's distinction between the two kinds of economy from discussions at the time the *General Theory* was in gestation? Or did he get it from his own reading of Marx, which I had always assumed to have been minimal? Anyway, it shows that he had an eye for what is important in Marx far keener than any of the other bourgeois economists."

To this Joan Robinson replied in her usual terse style (March 11): "I also was surprised at the note about Keynes and Marx. Keynes said to me that he used to try to get Sraffa to explain to him the meaning of labor value, etc., and recommend passages to read, but that he could never make out what it was about."

Subsequent inquiries have yielded no further information on how Keynes came to be acquainted with the Marxian formulas. Since his reading of Marx was obviously casual, to say the least, it seems possible that he may have come across them in a secondary source. In any case the fact that they made an impression on him is clear evidence of a certain similarity between his own and Marx's way of conceptualizing the capitalist economy.

treat from the one and only serious attempt of bourgeois economics to come to grips with the general crisis of late capitalism.

Under these circumstances it was only natural that critical thought in the field of economics should become more and more exclusively the realm of what might be called the Marxist opposition. The profession, having abandoned or denatured Keynes, purged itself of all radical impulses and soon moved sharply to the right, reviving two time-honored fallacies: Say's law of markets and the quantity theory of money, now respectively rechristened supply-side economics and monetarism.

Against this background we have the phenomenon of Robert L. Heilbroner. Heilbroner did his undergraduate work at Harvard in the late 1930s when Keynesian influence was at its peak, with Harvard professor Alvin Hansen, one of Heilbroner's teachers, being generally considered Keynes's most influential American follower. He went on to do graduate work at the New School in New York where he came under the influence of Adolph Lowe, one of the distinguished German emigres who then dominated the New School Graduate Faculty. Lowe, still alive and now in his 90s, is not easy to classify, but he was clearly both on the left of the German economics profession under the Weimar Republic and an outstanding teacher. Thus though exposed to mainstream orthodoxy at both Harvard and the New School, Heilbroner was never in any danger of becoming one of its devotees. He had come to see economics not as a narrowly circumscribed "science" but in the tradition of Adam Smith and Karl Marx as an important part of humanity's quest to understand its achievements, its hopes, and its limitations. This orientation was most clearly reflected in his first and still probably his best-known book, *The Worldly Philosophers,* a uniquely readable introduction to the history of economic thought which has brought enlightenment and pleasure to several generations of students fortunate enough to have had it on their assigned reading lists.

For reasons that should now be obvious, Heilbroner was always something of an anomaly in the American economics profession. A first-rate teacher and a prolific writer, he rose rapidly to become the holder of the endowed Norman Thomas chair in economics at the New School. But he was all along considered an outsider by the neoclassical faithful, and he was careful to keep his distance from the Marxist critics. In recent years, however, and especially since the onset of stagflation in the mid-1970s, Heilbroner, no doubt like many others, has come to feel increasingly unhappy about the state of the profession. But if the accredited economists don't have the answers, which are obviously more urgently needed than ever, then maybe the Marxist alternative should be taken more seriously. It must have been thoughts of this kind that led Heilbroner in recent years to write a series of books which by their very titles reflect both a troubled state of mind and a search for clarification outside the confines of the conventional wisdom: *An Inquiry into the Human Prospect* (1974), *Business Civilization in Decline* (1976), *Beyond Boom and Crash* (1978), *Marxism: For and Against* (1980), and *The Nature and Logic of Capitalism* (1985).

The last and latest of this series is, to my mind, by far the most interesting from a Marxist point of view. By this I do not mean to imply that Heilbroner has become a Marxist. For me a Marxist is anyone who identifies him- or herself as such, from which it follows of course that there are good Marxists, bad Marxists, and a variety of intermediate types of Marxists. By this standard Heilbroner is not a Marxist, at least on the evidence of this book. But what is important for present purposes is that the book places him squarely within the Marxist universe of discourse, a fact he himself recognizes on the very first page of the preface. I quote:

> Is this a Marxist view of capitalism? I am myself at a loss to give a clearcut answer to the question in view of the sprawling and disorganized state of what passes as a "Marxist" approach to social inquiry in general, or capitalism in particular. Much therefore depends on one's knowledge of that vast and ill-defined effort. For readers who will encounter for the first time the overall vision of capitalism that emerges in these pages, Marx's thought will no doubt appear as the single most pervasive and important influence. For others, more familiar with that thought and its elaboration within contemporary social science and history, what is apt to be noticeable are the distances and differences that separate my vision from that of much Marxian scholarship today and from Marx himself.

Speaking as an unambiguous Marxist in the sense indicated above, I take this to be an invitation to discuss Heilbroner's "overall vision of capitalism" as well as some of the "distances and differences" which he sees as separating it from that of Marx and present-day followers of Marx.

Let me begin by heartily agreeing with Heilbroner that all the great economists—and the same could be said of social analysts in general—start from and build on a vision of the social system with which they are concerned, a vision that embraces the major social actors, the form and content of their interrelations and interactions, the dynamics of the system, and its historical destiny. Classical political economy from Adam Smith through John Stuart Mill had such a vision, and so of course did Marx. Among twentieth-century figures, only Schumpeter and Keynes qualify for inclusion in the list. The neoclassical school that totally dominates bourgeois economics in our time may be said to have a vision too, but this vision is so totally dominated by the spirit of apologetics that it turns into a pale and lifeless caricature of the historical reality it purports to reflect: instead of classes in collision and conflict, the actors are powerless individuals seeking to maximize their utilities through the medium of impersonal markets; in this fantasy world they are all equal and have no interrelations outside the market; the dynamics of the system is to move, more or less smoothly and expeditiously, toward a state of general equilibrium; the system's historical destiny is to reproduce the status quo ad infinitum. Such a vision may give rise to intriguing intellectual games, but it doesn't help anyone to understand the world we live in or the problems we face.

Heilbroner rejects this neoclassical vision, and he goes a long way toward replacing it with Marx's vision. This, in my opinion, is the decisive feature of the book and what makes it a potentially important contribution to the contemporary social sciences. If teachers and students alike would read it carefully, think about it seriously, and ask themselves whether its central message does or does not accord with their own experience and what they observe around them in their everyday lives, I believe many of them would be ripe for conversion to new and more fruitful ways of ordering and analyzing the materials they seek to deal with in their work and studies.

The key to understanding capitalism, as Heilbroner sees it, is the process of capital accumulation, M-C-M′ in Marx's famous shorthand.* Comparing capitalism with the human organism, we could say that M-C-M′ is the heartbeat that pumps the system's monetary lifeblood through its arteries and veins. In the one case as in the other, the health of the system depends on the proper functioning of the heart: irregularity or weakness causes systemic illness and in extreme cases threatens life itself.

Once the centrality of M-C-M′ is duly recognized, it is but a short and hardly avoidable step to seeing it not only as a convenient economic conceptualization (the way Keynes saw it), or even as simply the engine of the economy, but as the dominant force in shaping the system's political, ideological, and cultural aspects. Heilbroner takes this step with full awareness of its far-reaching significance. What he had defined at the outset as "the object of my inquiries," i.e., the question *what is capitalism?*, thus yields not the description of an economic system—although that too is included—but the complex, many-sided, seminal concept of "The Regime of Capital" (the title of the third chapter). This, I think, is Heilbroner's unique achievement, unrivalled in its way by any other contemporary social analyst.

There is no need here to follow Heilbroner in his exploration of the impact of the regime of capital in the areas of politics and ideology—subjects of the fourth and fifth chapters respectively. Here he is on more familiar ground: and while what he has to say is for the most part interesting and helpful, it does not pose significant new questions from the standpoint of the book's central theme, i.e., in the words of its title, the "nature and logic of capitalism." I would go further and add that as long as the author remains on the highly abstract plane of capital and capitalism *in general,* as he does throughout most of the

* Those not familiar with Marx's introduction of the formula should consult *Capital,* Vol. 1, Part II ("The Transformation of Money into Capital"), a condensed thirty-four pages that constitutes one of the highlights of the whole work.

book, the range of questions inviting attention is rather restricted. It is only when we move to lower levels of abstraction, specifying capitalism's historical and spatial dimensions, that we open the floodgates to new and, not surprisingly, difficult and controversial questions. It is in this context that we encounter the "distances and differences" that separate Heilbroner from Marx and various of Marx's followers.

It is of course impossible in a short essay to go deeply into questions that arise as we move from the abstract to the (more) concrete. But it is also impossible to avoid them altogether, for that, in my opinion, would be to leave the whole discussion of the nature and logic of capitalism in a truncated and hence not only unsatisfactory but basically misleading condition. What follows is therefore an attempt in desperate brevity to direct attention to one extremely important problem area that emerges when we take leave of the abstract level of capital in general and enter that of capital in history. This is the uneven development of capitalism.

Heilbroner speaks of the origins of capitalism in terms of the formation of the proletariat as the necessary complement to the capital (self-expanding value) amassed through plunder and trade (Marx's "primitive accumulation"). But he does not take account of the historical fact that this process originated in a small part of the globe (Western Europe) and from the outset at the expense of much larger areas on other continents which came under its domination and control. Thus, practically from the beginning of its existence as a viable social formation, capitalism was divided into two parts: one that has increasingly come to be called the "center," where the logic of capital unfolded in a relatively unobstructed fashion; and the other, the "periphery," where expanding capital met a variety of precapitalist formations.

It had been originally supposed by Marx and his early followers that this encounter between expanding capital and precapitalist formations would result in the destruction of the latter and the incorporation of the vacated space into the unified regime of capital at large. This had indeed been the experience in the original Western European centers of capitalism, and it was logical to assume that the same process of destruction-and-absorption would continue until the whole globe had been transformed into one homogeneous world capitalist system. But this is not what happened. Instead, capital expanding from the center met with various types of resistance on the one hand and with dazzlingly lucrative opportunities on the other. The result was that destruction-and-absorption gave way to a process of dominating-remolding-and-exploiting. The division of capitalism into center and periphery thus turned out not to be a mere transitory phase in the overall history of capitalism but rather to be the lasting and increasingly deeply entrenched form of the system's global structure. And this brought with it profound modifications, not indeed in the nature of capitalism but certainly in its logic.

All of this is missing from Heilbroner's story. Whenever he needs to refer to a concrete capitalism, it is always Europe, the United States, and occasionally Japan that provide his examples—in other words, what are nowadays usually called the advanced or developed capitalist countries of the West. There is no hint of their having existed from the beginning of the capitalist era right down to the present in a close symbiotic relationship with the less developed and underdeveloped countries of the South and East. I feel pretty sure that Heilbroner would not deny the profound importance that this relationship has had for all parts of the capitalist world, and it is of course an accepted principle that book reviewers should not chide authors for choosing to write on some subjects and not on others. Still I think it is entirely legitimate to criticize an author who chooses a subject—as Heilbroner did when he decided to write on the "nature and logic of capitalism"—and then leaves out considerations that are not only important but indispensable for an understanding of key aspects of the chosen subject.

This is not the place to elaborate on this theme.* But I do

* Readers might be tempted to conclude from what is said above that Marx's own vision of capitalism did not include the division into developed and underdeveloped parts and the consequences flowing therefrom. This is only partly true. While *Capital* is focused on developed capitalism (as exemplified by England), all three volumes are full of historical references to the relations between capitalist and precapitalist formations, and in the last decade of his life Marx's mostly unpublished notes and writings clearly

want to point out certain respects in which, at least to my way of thinking, Heilbroner's vision of capitalism is flawed by the failure to take account of capitalism's two faces, development and underdevelopment, bound together as they are in indissoluble unity.

Marx taught that capitalism is an inherently self-destructive system that must sooner or later be replaced by a new and different form of society. This of course would not happen automatically: as in the case of earlier profound social transformations, it would come about as the result of a revolution, which in this case Marx believed would be led by the proletariat in the advanced capitalist countries. By the end of the nineteenth century, however, it was already clear that this would not happen. The Western working classes had become basically reformist, concentrating their political energies on improving their lot within the system rather than on overthrowing it. To many, both inside and outside the Marxist camp, this failure of the proletariat to carry out its supposed revolutionary mission was also the failure of Marxism itself and should logically have been followed by its disintegration and downfall. But this also did not happen. As it turned out, the twentieth century has produced more, and more profound, revolutions than any previous century. Most of them have been avowedly anticapitalist, and the more important ones have taken place under Marxist leadership. Today, more than a hundred years after Marx's death, we can say without exaggeration that Marxism has become more truly universal in its appeal than any other body of ideas, secular or religious, in the history of the human race.

---

show that he was moving away from his earlier belief in the tendency of capitalist expansion to create a homogenized capitalist world. (See Teodor Shanin, ed., *Late Marx and the Russian Road: Marx and the "Peripheries of Capitalism,"* Monthly Review Press, 1984.) Nevertheless, it is true that for more than half a century after Marx's death, his followers continued to hold, and indeed to rigidify, what by the end of the nineteenth century had become the orthodox view of the European socialist parties. It was only after the Second World War, with the spread of Marxist ideas in the third world, that the view of capitalism as a dialectical unity of developed center and underdeveloped periphery can be said to have become a central aspect of the Marxist vision. Paul Baran's *Political Economy of Growth* (Monthly Review Press, 1957) played a key role in making explicit what many third world Marxists were feeling but still had not been able to articulate in a theoretically convincing formulation.

How explain this paradox—the failure of the proletariat and the flourishing of Marxism? Basically, the answer is that the revolutionary center of gravity in the capitalist system shifted from its developed to its underdeveloped part. The penetration of the latter by the regime of capital created a mass of suffering humanity conforming closely to Marx and Engels's description of "the fully developed proletariat" (in their joint work, *The Holy Family,* written in 1843) as those whose "living conditions represent the focal point of all inhuman conditions in modern society."

The revolutions powered by what may be called this "new proletariat" of course have their own characteristics, different in many ways from the kind of revolutions Marxists had so long expected. They occur not in the most advanced capitalist countries but in the system's "weakest links" (Lenin) and inevitably first take the form of national liberation struggles. Moreover, since the economies inherited from the capitalist era are both weak and terribly deformed, they have the added task of accomplishing much that has already been accomplished in the developed countries. Their typical form became clear only after the Second World War, but in retrospect we can see that the Russian Revolution, despite the role of the industrial proletariat in the overthrow of the tsarist regime, had more in common with the third world revolutions of our time than with the revolutions of traditional Marxist theory.

Why do I raise these questions in the present context? Because it seems to me that they are inescapably part and parcel of the "logic of capitalism," and that their total absence from Heilbroner's argument is a good indication of the extent to which his vision of capitalism, for all its power at the abstract level of capital in general, falls short of providing an adequate framework within which to analyze the revolutionary and counterrevolutionary struggles that are increasingly putting their stamp on the historical period in which we are living.

# *International Finance and National Power*

International finance strikes most people as a realm of mystery. When even specialists are unable to unravel the tangled web of international money and banking, it is hardly surprising that the rest of us throw up our hands at trying to penetrate these knotty and puzzling subjects. The technical aspects of the international money market are indeed complex, but getting bogged down in the day-to-day details only adds to the confusion. For the basic issues in this area are not so much technical as political: it is crucial to understand that international finance veils a struggle for *power and wealth.* In the realm of international relations, wealth enhances a nation's power, and power is a means of expanding a nation's wealth.

The international money market is, in a sense, the nerve center of the world capitalist system. And it is there that each of the leading nations, in tandem with finance capital, maneuvers to acquire ascendancy or, at the very least, to retain the power it has already acquired. This becomes clear if we view the problem historically, against the background of changes during the past 125 years, which can be divided for the present purpose into three stages: the years of the gold standard, the era between the two world wars, and the post-Second World War decades.

According to conventional wisdom, international economic relations were automatically regulated by the gold standard from approximately the mid-nineteenth century to the First World War. Our economics textbooks explain with great precision and logic the mechanism by which the gold standard

This article originally appeared in the October 1983 issue of *Monthly Review*.

achieved equilibrium and preserved stability of exchange rates during the nineteenth and early twentieth centuries. The facts, however, are quite different. It is true that a good measure of success was achieved in those years in maintaining exchange-rate stability, but it was a stability confined to the advanced capitalist countries. As explained by Professor Triffin:

> This success . . . was limited to the more advanced countries, which formed the core of the system, and to those closely linked to them by political, as well as economic and financial ties. The exchange rates of other currencies—particularly in Latin America—fluctuated widely, and depreciated enormously, over the period. This contrast between the "core" countries and those of the "periphery" can be largely explained by the cyclical pattern of capital movements and terms of trade, which contributed to stability in the first group, and to instability in the second. (Robert Triffin, *Our International Monetary System: Yesterday, Today, and Tomorrow* [New York: Random House, 1968], p. 13)

Moreover, even in the case of the core countries, stability was achieved not through the automatic mechanism of the gold standard, but because of Great Britain's dominant role in international finance. It was not the gold standard but Britain that ruled the roost.

The advantages that Britain enjoyed during most of the nineteenth century were its overwhelming military (naval) superiority, its vast colonial empire, and its leading position as manufacturer, trader, and banker. This unique combination of factors led to London's becoming the financial center of the capitalist world. Britain's dominance before the First World War has been effectively summarized in a classic study of the gold standard:

> The world's foreign exchange markets were interconnected through London, and in many instances remittance from one market to another was habitually made in sterling, in preference to direct remittance. London was the world center for the clearance of foreign exchange transactions, though smaller patterns centered directly around Paris, Berlin, and New York were woven into the main design of the picture. In this prewar system of foreign exchange markets all countries had a substantial interest in keeping their particular currencies as stable as possible in terms of sterling, and their success in doing so contributed to the stability of their currencies in terms of one another.

One reason for this interest in keeping London exchange stable was that the world-wide price-making forces of primary raw materials were brought to a focus in world markets in London and Liverpool. British consumer demand was a dominant influence in the formation of many of these prices, of which the price of wool is a good example. In addition, the British view of the prospects of primary commodities had a great psychological influence in other countries, and throughout the continent buyers and sellers followed the British traders' lead. The world prices established in the British market were a common element in the price structures of many countries. Their fluctuations in response to world-wide supply and demand forces directly influenced the incomes of large groups of producers in many countries, and consequently the demand for many products not traded in internationally. They affected domestic costs of production. The international influence of the London or Liverpool price of many important commodities was therefore a factor tending to prevent substantial divergence in the movements of general prices of countries adhering to the international gold standard. (William Adams Brown, Jr., *The International Gold Standard Reinterpreted 1914-1934* [New York: National Bureau of Economic Research, 1940], Vol. II, pp. 774-75)

This unique role of the London money market—its influence on world prices and on the internal price structure of other countries—was bolstered by its ability to export capital. The flow of credit from London, and not the mechanics of the gold standard, cushioned imbalances arising from economic transactions among the leading nations. And the ability to perform this function was in turn based on Britain's hegemonic position. It was the latter which enabled Britain to move capital abroad beyond what its gold reserves and trade balance would in the normal course of events support. This foreign lending capacity was enlarged by two factors: (1) the acceptance by other countries of sterling as a reserve currency; and (2) the large deposits kept in London banks by members of its empire, countries that borrowed heavily in England, and allies that relied on British military support.

Britain's domination of international finance was for all practical purposes undisputed during most of the nineteenth century, but this situation began to change as the century drew to a close. Its supremacy on the seas was challenged by the emergence of powerful navies built by other imperialist powers, and its lead in manufacturing and trade was cut into by the rise of competing industrial nations. Nevertheless, despite a gradual loss of absolute hegemony, London remained the world center of finance until the First World War. In part, this was due to the sophisticated banking institutions created during earlier years and to the continuous inflow of profits from foreign investment. But more important were the advantages arising from Britain's long-standing colonial possessions. When competition from other industrialized nations began to hurt, Britain was able to shift exports to its colonies. And control over the colonies, notably India, provided a source of financial strength:

> India had assumed in the twenty-five years under discussion [1890-1914] the role of a protagonist of the international settlements system: her trade surplus with the rest of the world and her trade deficit with England allowed the latter to square her international settlements on current account. This enabled her to use the income from her overseas investment for further investment abroad, and to give back to the international monetary system the liquidity she had absorbed as investment income.
>
> This, however, was not the only reason why India had an important place in the international monetary system. The reserves on which the Indian monetary system was based provided a large *masse de manoeuvre* which British monetary authorities could use to supplement their own reserves and to keep London the center of the international monetary system. (Marcello de Cecco, *Money and Empire, the International Gold Standard, 1890-1914* [Oxford: Basil Blackwell, 1974], p. 62)

Although London remained in the driver's seat, there was growing uneasiness in British corridors of power as other money market centers began to gather strength in the years preceding the First World War. U.S. banking power was on the rise and the U.S. Treasury (along with the banks) stockpiled gold at a furious rate. Dependence on London was becoming increasingly irksome to U.S. financiers, but in the absence of a central bank and other needed institutional arrangements, the New York money market had little opportunity before 1914 to free itself from this yoke. On the other hand, the huge absorption of gold by the United States was potentially a menace. By 1910 the United States controlled one third of all the gold held by monetary authorities. The British managed the gold market and held onto their predominance with the use of a relatively small stock of gold: controlling less than 4 percent of all gold reserves held by monetary authorities. The U.S. gold reserves were for the moment idle, but they hung like a sword of Damocles over the world's financial system.

France too became a major gold holder, second only to the United States, and likewise a potential threat to British ascendancy. In addition, Paris became an important exporter of capital, for political as well as economic advantage. Its expanding banking system competed for deposits by foreign governments, once Britain's preserve. Yet troublesome as the emerging New York and Paris financial centers were, the most pressing and urgent threat came from Germany. It should be recalled that the practically universal use of sterling in international trade was a principal component of Britain's financial sway, and it was precisely into this strategic sphere that Germany began to penetrate, with the mark evolving as an alternative to the pound. The Deutsche Bank conducted "a stubborn fight for the introduction of the mark acceptance in overseas trade in place of the hitherto universal sterling bill . . . this fight lasted for decades and when the war came, a point had just been reached at which the mark acceptance in direct transactions with German firms had partially established itself alongside the pound sterling." (H. Parker Willis and B. H. Beckhart, *Foreign Banking Systems* [New York: Henry Holt, 1929], p. 710)

Rivalry among the advanced capitalist nations was the name of the game in the upsurge of imperialism toward the end of the nineteenth century. This was evident in the strife for colonies and spheres of influence, the intensified competition in world trade, the growth of protectionism, and the arms race. And to this must be added measures taken by rival nations early in the twentieth century to unseat Britain from its unique privileged position in the monetary field. In this regard, Germany was the main threat to Britain's wealth and economic security. As one economic historian put it: "It seems probable that if war had not come in 1914, London would have had to share with Germany the regulatory power over world trade and economic development which it had exercised so markedly in the nineteenth century." (J. B. Condliffe, *The Commerce of Nations* [New York: Norton, 1950], p. 378)

Whether regulatory power could have been shared for long by two rival nations is highly dubious. In the very nature of the case, the benefits accruing to one party in the exercise of such power would harm the other. A more-or-less equal distribution of regulatory power between rival nations would tend sooner or later to lead to an economic, and possibly a shooting war. And this was indeed one of the underlying causes of the First World War which drastically changed the entire pre-existing balance of forces and in the process produced havoc in the international monetary system.

The finances of Britain, France, and Germany were undermined by the war. Britain and France were faced with huge debts, while Germany was saddled with an enormous reparations burden. Britain, in addition, lost a source of foreign income because it had had to sell off foreign investments to pay for munitions purchases. On the other hand, the international financial position of the United States began to measure up to its industrial strength. It had financed the Allies and was now in the envious position of a creditor nation. The destruction of industrial and agricultural capacity in Europe opened up opportunities for the expansion of U.S. exports, and the huge stockpile of gold amassed in earlier years stood the country in good stead. On top of all this, the passage of the Federal Reserve Act in 1913 created an effective central bank and removed earlier barriers to the development of international banking.

The shifting national fortunes created a new constellation of power at the heart of world capitalism. Britain was no longer able to control international monetary affairs as in the past. But it did retain its empire, its international banking network, and its traditional trade channels. As a result, the pound continued to be used as a reserve currency, though much less so than in prewar years. Increasingly, London had to contend with the growing use of the U.S. dollar as a competing reserve currency. Instead of its earlier hegemony, Britain had to cope with the rivalry of a vigorous new challenger.

As economic recovery took over after the war, the Western countries attempted a return to the gold standard and more-or-less fixed exchange rates. But the resulting stability was short-lived. Neither the United States nor Britain alone had sufficient resources to dominate the international monetary system. The power structure was a divided one, with each nation striving mightily to protect its own interests at the expense of the interests of its rivals. As a consequence, the shaky stability of the mid-twenties, resting as it did on a weak and unreliable foundation, came tumbling down with the crash of 1929. And the fragility of the international monetary system of the 1920s contributed in its turn to the depth and length of the ensuing depression.

The Great Depression brought with it a slew of bank failures and chaos in the international economy. World exports dropped precipitously, falling 25 percent between 1929 and 1933, and the export of capital dried up. Countries in the periphery went into a tailspin as the demand for their exports shrank and foreign capital was no longer available to help them cope, if only temporarily, with their balance-of-payments difficulties. The international monetary system simply disintegrated.

In these conditions it was inevitable that economic warfare among the leading capitalist nations should become the order of the day. In this bitter struggle, the following five currency and trading blocs were involved: (1) the sterling bloc: Britain, its colonies and dominions (except Canada), and a number of independent countries that in the past had strong trading and banking ties to Britain; (2) the U.S. dollar area: the United States, countries in North and South America, and U.S. possessions; (3) the "gold bloc" led by France and including Switzerland, Belgium, the Netherlands, Italy, and Poland; (4) the German sphere of influence based on bilateral trade and currency agreements between Nazi Germany and Central and Eastern European countries; (5) the yen bloc: Japan, its colonies and newly conquered territories, and a number of other Asian countries. The common feature of each of these groupings was the binding of relatively weaker, dependent nations to a core country.

Some attempts at reconciliation among the blocs were made in this period, notably the Tripartite Monetary Agreement of 1936 between France, England, and the United States. But that feeble arrangement did not lead, as intended, to the reconstitution of an international monetary order, and the dominant feature of the 1930s remained a stagnating world economy divided into contending blocs. What is especially noteworthy about these blocs, and the alliances formed among some of them, is that they pretty much prefigured the lineups of the belligerents in the Second World War.

The peace which followed the Second World War provided a new opportunity to unify the world capitalist system, this time under the leadership of the United States, which had again emerged a tower of industrial and financial strength among devastated combatants. But whereas after the First World War the United States was a novice at the game and had to struggle to find a place for itself at the top, this was no longer the case after the Second World War. For all practical purposes Great Britain had been knocked out: to finance the war it had consumed a good deal of its capital, again sold off its foreign investments, gone heavily into debt, and needed to borrow still more to get back on its feet. The United States, on the other hand, not only stood out as a creditor nation in a sea of debtors but also possessed the most powerful military force and the largest industrial capacity. In short, the United States was in a position to call the tune.

The architects of the international economic system which emerged from the Second World War were haunted by memories of the disarray among the major financial powers which characterized the 1930s: growing protectionism, moribund international capital flows, constantly fluctuating exchange rates, and trade and currency wars. The new order designed to overcome these evils consisted of three principal elements: liberalization of trade through removal or reduction of tariffs and other barriers to the free flow of goods (GATT); creation of credit to stimulate development in the third world and hence demand for exports from the industrialized nations (World Bank); and stabilization of exchange rates (IMF). The primacy of the United States was directly or indirectly recognized in each of these new institutional arrangements, most notably in the fact that the new currency parities were expressed in a gold unit equal to the official gold price of the dollar ($35 per fine ounce). What this meant, in effect, was that all other currencies were tied to the dollar and the dollar itself to gold. The stage was thus set for the dollar to become the universal currency.

The innovations were geared to a revitalization and expansion of world trade which was expected to, and in fact for some two decades did, buttress a new long wave of prosperity. Underlying all this was the assumption that harmony of interests among the leading nations could be achieved and maintained. In the circumstances of the time, this was not too fanciful a notion. Frictions arising from conflicts of interest among the ruling classes of different nations were of course ever present. Yet in the aftermath of war there were reasons for a degree of harmony to exist, some of them associated with the presumed self-interest of the capitalist nations and others imposed by the urgent need of war-torn, resource-depleted countries for U.S. assistance. There was also a strongly felt need, in view of the expansion of the socialist world, to prevent further revolutions, even including ones which seemed to be threatening in some of the weaker developed capitalist countries such as France and Italy. Finally, new and more reliable means of control over restive countries in the third world were urgently required. For all these reasons the colossal U.S. military machine, straddling the globe, was perceived by other capitalist nations to be a crucial defender of their own most vital interests, while from an immediate economic standpoint, they desperately needed U.S. loans and grants to rebuild their treasuries and to get reconstruction under way.

Given these conditions of generalized dependence, "harmonious" submission to the will of the United States was the natural consequence. This is not to say, however, that all the powers were happy about every aspect of the new order, especially the adoption of the U.S. dollar as the universal currency. Still, even this latter did not seem too onerous or dangerous in the light of the size of Washington's gold reserve. Dollar convertibility appeared to be well protected by the 70 percent of the world's monetary gold stock resting in this country's vaults. Finally, there was a widespread belief—or at least hope—that the leading powers, having digested the lessons of the 1930s, would become self-disciplined and cooperative, taking their lumps when necessary for the good of the community of nations. Countries with a persistent surplus or deficit in their balance of payments, for example, would be expected to change their policies to restore equilibrium.

The system did work for nearly two decades. World trade expanded vigorously. After some initial postwar adjustments, exchange rates of the core countries remained relatively stable. (This was not true for the periphery where, as in the past, devaluations remained the norm.) Increasingly, however, the contradictions inherent in the new arrangements rose to the surface. Paradoxically, it was reliance on U.S. militray power as the protector of the capitalist world which generated the conditions that eventually led to increasing disharmony. The outflow of dollars from the United States to pay for its worldwide military machine, the major wars in Korea and Vietnam, and large-scale military and economic aid to client states generated severe strains in the U.S. balance of payments. Relations between the United States and the rest of the world were also thrown out of kilter by the export of capital associated with the mushrooming of U.S. multinational corporations—itself a byproduct of the disproportionate concentration of economic power in this country. The net result was a growing deficit in the U.S. balance of payments, beginning in the early 1950s, that ultimately led to the disintegration of the postwar international monetary system.

In the normal course of events, a country can manage with a balance-of-payments deficit as long as it has a sufficient reserve of gold or convertible currencies to cover the deficit. After the reserves are exhausted, relief may come from borrowing abroad or attracting foreign investment. But such "remedies" only intensify the underlying problem: bankers have to be repaid with interest, and foreign investors bring their profits back home, sooner or later. A country with a persistent deficit has to reduce imports and try to expand exports by cutting wages and other costs. The cost of reducing the country's balance of payments thus turns out to be a reduction in the people's living standards and economic stagnation.

If this is the expected consequence of a persistent balance-of-payments deficit, how does it happen that the U.S. economy, despite cyclical ups and downs, has been able to continue growing through some three decades of deficits? The answer lies in the nature of the postwar system we have been discussing. The Bretton Woods agreements made the dollar "as good as gold." For a long time U.S. deficits were needed and welcomed. An expanding global economy required expanding reserves of universal money, and the dollar filled the bill. But as the flood of dollars grew, responding *not* to the need for more reserves but to the requirements of the United States as the hegemonic power, harmony gradually gave way to its opposite. The other advanced capitalist countries found themselves with more dollars than they could use or wanted. One result was inflation of their domestic money supplies and the growth of the uncontrolled Eurodollar market. In an attempt to slow down the process, they converted part of their reserves into gold. This led Nixon in 1971 to suspend the convertibility of dollars into gold, an act which was soon followed by two devaluations of the dollar and the end of any semblance of a regime of stable exchange rates.

One might suppose that this would have sounded the death knell of the privileged position of the U.S. dollar, that a continuation of U.S. deficits after 1971 would necessarily lead to what was described above as the normal course of events to be expected from the persistence of deficits. But U.S. deficits have in fact persisted and indeed have grown, without the United States having been forced to suffer the consequences meted out by the "laws" of economics to lesser nations.

One cannot conclude from this that nothing basic has changed since 1971 or that the present situation of persistent deficits can continue indefinitely. What one can conclude is that important changes are certainly taking place, that we are clearly in a transition period, but that no one can yet tell for sure where we are going or how long it will take to get there.

The United States is still the richest and most powerful capitalist country, and the dollar is still the nearest thing there is to a universal currency. These were the solid foundations of the pre-1971 system. What has changed is not that the foundations are no longer in place but that they are no longer solid. Other capitalist centers, most notably Japan and West Germany, have been gaining in power relative to the United States since as far back as the Korean war.* Most central banks still hold the largest part of their reserves in dollars, but the proportion held in yen and marks has been steadily inching up in recent years. It is not in any country's interest to challenge the present hierarchy of wealth and power at this stage: the result would be chaos, not a new and more stable hierarchy. But the balance is shifting, and there may well come a time, perhaps sooner than we now think, when quantity will change into quality as it did after the two world wars (not necessarily as the result of war) and we will be faced with not merely a changing but a decisively new situation.

Meanwhile, the key to understanding developments in international power relations is to analyze the way the rival nations maneuver to strengthen their competitive positions for the struggles that lie ahead.

Conflicts of interest have surfaced more and more since the end of the 1960s as the capitalist world edged into a stage of stagnation. Retardation of growth combined with two severe downturns sharpened the competitive drives of all the powers. While professing devotion to free trade, they have increasingly resorted to protectionist measures. Higher tariffs, new trade barriers, and old-fashioned import quotas are on the rise. So far, these restraints of trade have affected primarily the older and sicker industries. They contain, however, the seeds of possible future trade wars and rival trade blocs.

While protectionism is a form of economic struggle focused on particular industries and products, exchange rates are weapons in the wider struggle to protect and if possible improve a country's overall trade balance. Trying to manipulate exchange

---

* The impact of the Korean war on the countries that eventually became the major competitors of the United States is little recognized. Pursuit of the war required a rapid rebuilding of the U.S. arsenal. And that was accomplished with the assistance of purchases from Japan (associated with Japan's proximity to the theater of war) and Germany (due to its machine-building capability). The post-Korean war militarization and the program of stockpiling strategic war materials kept up imports from these countries. It was U.S. demand stemming from the war and its aftermath that sparked the Japanese and German "miracles." While the Korean war marked the origin of a change in power relations, the war in Vietnam put the finishing touch on the undisputed supremacy of the United States. The defeat of the United States in Vietnam raised questions in the minds of its allies about U.S. military invulnerability, and the economic strains of the war exposed its financial vulnerability.

rates in one's favor is a game only financially powerful nations can play. But today not even the United States has the resources to dominate foreign-exchange markets, now grown to fantastic proportions. On the one hand, the huge overhang of dollars abroad is a source of unrestrained speculation and a constant threat to whatever momentary stability may be achieved. On the other hand, the United States, unable to control the situation, stubbornly continues to pursue, and even intensify, imperialist policies which result in unending balance-of-payments deficits and hence an expanding outflow of dollars.

For the last couple of years U.S. administrations have found what seems to them a solution to this threatening contradiction. They have raised interest rates to unprecedentedly high levels, pulling vast amounts of money into the country and temporarily narrowing the payments gap—but also undermining the U.S. domestic economy and playing havoc with the economies of its capitalist allies and rivals.

In these circumstances the conflict between the United States and the other core countries overshadows a multitude of other strains and conflicts, such as those arising from Germany's drive for ascendancy in the European Common Market. Meanwhile, summit meetings of the Western world's heads of state come and go. But the disorder in international finance, with its growing potential for a major disruption in what might still be called an international monetary system, remains.

# *The Two Faces of Third World Debt*

> **Falstaff: "I can get no remedy against the consumption of the purse: borrowing only lingers and lingers it out, but the disease is incurable."**
>
> ***King Henry IV, Part II***

The tremors that shook the financial world during 1982 and most of 1983 have for the time being subsided. But the ensuing calm is an uneasy one: clearly, the crisis has merely been postponed to another day.

The sense of panic among the financiers and governments of the leading capitalist nations is not the product of idle rumors or vague fears. It has been obvious for some time that the vast expansion of third world debt would sooner or later create serious problems for the international bankers. But the outsize profits to be made in the third world have been too tempting to be resisted by even the most prudent of bankers. The chickens began to come home to roost in 1982. In that year, 22 countries were forced to negotiate debt rescheduling because they could not meet their contractual payments. And it is evident that the fat was indeed in the fire when the three largest third world debtors—Mexico, Brazil, and Argentina—let it be known that they did not have the foreign exchange to pay interest and amortization due on their loans.

A default by one or a combination of these countries, as will be shown below, could lead to the bankruptcy of some of the biggest U.S. banks. Default was avoided because of prompt and energetic rescue measures taken by the U.S. government,

This article originally appeared in the January 1984 issue of *Monthly Review*.

by central bankers, and by the Bank for International Settlements, the IMF, and the World Bank. One thing, however, needs to be clearly understood about these heroic efforts in the heartland of finance: it was the banks that were rescued, not Mexico, Brazil, Argentina, and the other potential defaulters. As a matter of fact, an essential feature of the whole rescue operation consisted of pushing the affected third world countries further down the road of debt enslavement, with a consequent imposition of severe economic contraction and a decline in the already miserable living standards of the masses. Neither was the financial system of the imperialist countries strengthened: a crucial aspect of the rescue operation was a continued increase in third world debt and with it enhanced vulnerability of the international banks. On the other hand, the bankers have done well for themselves, at least for the time being. Not only was their skin saved, but they have managed to use the crisis to squeeze even more profits out of the third world.

Underlying all this is the simple fact that debt, like drugs, is addictive. The more you borrow, the more you need to borrow. A simple arithmetic example (Table 1) explains the logic

*Table 1*

*Net capital flow if $1,000 is borrowed each year: loan to be repaid in 20 years with 10 percent interest*

| | *New borrowing* | *Debt service on accumulated debt* | | | *Net proceeds (1) – (4)* |
|---|---|---|---|---|---|
| *Year* | | *Interest* | *Amortization* | *Total* | |
| | *(1)* | *(2)* | *(3)* | *(4)* | *(5)* |
| 1st | $1,000 | $100 | $50 | $150 | $850 |
| 2nd | 1,000 | 195 | 100 | 295 | 705 |
| 3rd | 1,000 | 285 | 150 | 435 | 565 |
| 5th | 1,000 | 450 | 250 | 700 | 300 |
| 6th | 1,000 | 525 | 300 | 825 | 175 |
| 7th | 1,000 | 595 | 350 | 945 | 55 |
| 8th | 1,000 | 660 | 400 | 1,060 | – 60 |
| 10th | 1,000 | 775 | 500 | 1,275 | –275 |

of the process. We assume that a country obtains each year a foreign loan of $1,000, to be repaid in equal installments over 20 years plus 10 percent interest on the outstanding balance. The net result is shown in the last column. The amount left over after paying the accumulated debt service (return of principal plus interest) gets smaller and smaller each year. By the fifth year, $700 of the new loan is needed just to keep up service payments on the mounting debt. And by the eighth year, borrowing of $1,000 is insufficient to meet obligations on the past debt. Thus if a country's development strategy were to call for a net annual inflow of $1,000 of foreign money, an *increase* in the rate of borrowing would be needed. In other words, a *growing* volume of external debt would become a way of life. Moreover, even if the country wanted to abandon reliance on debt, it would be hard put to do so. For unless it had other means of obtaining foreign exchange (say, an expanding excess of exports over imports), it would still need to keep on borrowing. As shown in the example, in the eighth year $1,060 and in the tenth year $1,275 would have to be borrowed just to meet debt service obligations. And if in the meantime the interest rate on new debt should increase or exports should decline, still more borrowing would be called for.

The foregoing is of course a highly simplified example, but it isn't all that far removed from third world reality. Table 2 shows what has actually been happening to the debt of the third world. As can be seen in the last column, over 56 percent of the new debt undertaken in 1972 by the underdeveloped countries

*Table 2*
*Debt Service on External Debt of Underdeveloped Countries*

| Year | New borrowing | Debt service | Net proceeds (1) – (2) | Debt service as a percent of new borrowing $\frac{(2)}{(1)} \times 100$ |
|---|---|---|---|---|
| | Billions of dollars | | | |
| | (1) | (2) | (3) | (4) |
| 1972 | 21.3 | 12.0 | 9.3 | 56.3% |
| 1974 | 36.7 | 19.8 | 16.9 | 54.0 |
| 1976 | 49.9 | 26.1 | 23.8 | 52.3 |
| 1977 | 61.5 | 33.1 | 28.4 | 53.8 |
| 1978 | 80.7 | 47.9 | 32.8 | 59.4 |
| 1979 | 94.2 | 62.3 | 31.9 | 66.1 |
| 1980 | 94.9 | 70.4 | 24.5 | 74.2 |
| 1981 | 110.0 | 82.8 | 27.2 | 75.3 |

*Source:* The World Bank, *World Debt Tables, First Supplement,* May 1983.

as a whole was needed just to meet debt service obligations. By 1981 this figure climbed to 75 percent. Now look at the third column of the table, which shows what was left over from new borrowings after payment of debt service. The net proceeds did increase from 1972 to 1978, but that was because in contrast with our hypothetical example, new borrowing grew rapidly from year to year. And after 1978 the amount left over after payment of debt service *declined* each year, even though the amount newly borrowed kept on increasing.

There were three special reasons for this decline in net proceeds, each of which contributed to bringing the third world debt problem to the critical juncture of 1981-82. First, interest rates on new debt jumped substantially. Second, a larger portion of the new debt was short-term, with a consequent increase in annual amortization payments. And third, the banks, anticipating the approaching perils, began to slow down their lending.

The nature of the financial dependency of the periphery on the core extends beyond the issue of debt. This can be seen clearly from the data on the aggregate balance of payments of all Latin American countries (except Cuba). Table 3 summarizes the multitude of foreign transactions by Latin Ameri-

*Table 3*

*Balance of Payments on Current Account: Latin America (except Cuba)*

| | *1976* | *1977* | *1978* | *1979* | *1980* | *1981* |
|---|---|---|---|---|---|---|
| | | | *Billions of dollars* | | | |
| Merchandise trade (exports-imports) | - 1.9 | - 0.1 | - 3.2 | +0.2 | - 1.3 | - 2.1 |
| Net payments to foreign capital | - 9.5 | -11.2 | -13.5 | -17.4 | -22.5 | -31.5 |
| Freight & insurance | - 2.3 | - 2.8 | - 2.9 | - 3.1 | - 3.9 | - 4.1 |
| Dividends, interest, royalties, etc. | - 7.2 | - 8.4 | -10.6 | -14.3 | -18.6 | -27.4 |
| All other transactions on current account | +0.3 | - 0.2 | - 1.3 | - 2.1 | - 3.2 | - 5.2 |
| Balance on current account | -11.1 | -11.5 | -18.0 | -19.3 | -27.0 | -38.8 |

*Source:* Inter-American Development Bank, *Economic and Social Progress in Latin America, 1983 Report.*

can countries, other than capital movements (foreign investment, net new debt), in three categories: merchandise trade (exports minus imports); payments to foreign capital; and all other (a miscellany of services, such as tourism, and transfer of funds by migrant labor, missionaries, etc.) The table goes back only to 1976, but the situation it depicts is much older. The persistent deficit in the current balance of payments in Latin America and elsewhere in the third world has been chronic for decades. And the reason, obviously, is the tribute exacted by foreign capital. During the six years shown here, on the average 85 percent of the deficit was accounted for by the need for foreign exchange to pay shippers and insurance companies; dividends, royalties, etc. to multinational corporations and other foreign capitalists; and interest to international bankers.

These huge deficits on current account defines the bind in which Latin American and other third world countries find themselves. Obligations of this kind cannot be ignored or put off to another day. If they are not met promptly, trade will collapse; imports needed to feed the people and keep the wheels of industry turning will dry up. As long as their economies remain wrapped up in the imperialist network, they must obtain the foreign exchange needed to cover the deficits by attracting investment from multinational corporations and by borrowing from foreign banks. But that path leads to even greater deficits. Multinationals invest in order to obtain still more profits, and bankers demand interest. As a result, as we have seen, the deficits kept on growing until a critical point was reached, i.e., the point when the funds obtainable from foreign bankers began to dry up.

This was when the U.S. treasury and the international financial agencies (IMF, Bank for International Settlements, World Bank) jumped into the breach, supplying quick money to avoid immediate defaults and helping to arrange stretched-out schedules for repayment of principal. These stopgap measures provided what the international bankers needed: part of the risk was shifted to the public; and the international agencies applied strong-arm pressure to force potentially defaulting nations to adopt policies of reducing imports and restricting mass consumption. This in turn generated a climate in which the banks were once again prepared to resume their lending operations.

Characteristically, the international bankers made the most of their improved prospects. They collected handsome fees for renegotiating old loans and raised the interest charges on renegotiated and new loans. This contrasts strikingly with their practice when faced with near-bankrupt corporations. In such cases, the banks generally make concessions by reducing interest rates below prevailing market rates. This they consider prudent since what they fear most is that the troubled firms will actually fold up and their debt will be uncollectible. Governments, on the other hand do not become bankrupt, so why not squeeze out still more profits while the getting is good?

The point of view of the bankers was clearly stated by Willard Butcher, chairman of Chase Manhattan, when Mexico's inability to pay shook the markets:

> Mexico owes $85 billion. Is Mexico worth $85 billion? Of course it is. It has oil exports of $15 to $20 billion. It has gold, silver, copper. Has all that disappeared over the past week? I expect to be repaid my Mexican debt. (*Euromoney,* October 1982, p. 19)

But how to make sure that the benefit of those resources will accrue to the bankers and not to the Mexicans and other third world peoples? That is where the international agencies come in. They are the ones who coordinate the programs, oversee the domestic policies, and keep the debtors in line to protect the interests of the bankers. The following from the *New York Times* (September 19, 1983) sums it up:

> "The IMF is certainly running the show for the sovereign debtors," said Penelope Hartland-Thunberg, senior fellow at the Georgetown Center for Strategic and International Studies.
>
> C. Fred Bergsten, director of the Institute for International Economics, called the peripatetic teams of [World Bank] and [IMF] officials "the new proconsuls," alluding to the governors of the Roman Empire, saying that they represent the world's "increasingly centralized economic management."

The real question is, economic management for what purpose? It is obviously not to help third world countries restructure their societies to become more self-reliant, to raise their living standards, and to free themselves from debt slavery. On the contrary, the aim is to keep the imperialist system as now constituted going as long as possible. And that means, in turn, protecting the profits of the banks and the multinationals and maintaining an environment in which these profits can grow still further. To accomplish this the IMF has been imposing its standard prescription, except that the requirements have become more extreme in keeping with the severity of the crisis: devaluation of currencies, liberalization of trade, and reduction of public spending.

Devaluations, however, do not help promote the better utilization of resources needed to escape the debt trap. This is due to the inflexible and backward production structures of the underdeveloped countries. By raising the cost of imports, devaluations make it more difficult to overcome the bottlenecks and rigidities that constrain productive capacity. At the same time they add to inflationary pressures that worsen the unequal distribution of income and reduce internal markets. Trade liberalization weakens local industry and opens the gates wider for entry of the multinationals. Finally, the reduction in public spending means primarily drastic cuts in health, education, and welfare spending. Neither the international agencies nor the domestic ruling classes want government budgets to be reduced by limiting spending on the military and police, for these are more than ever needed to control the unemployed and hungry masses. The overall impact of the imposed discipline is seen in the results in Latin America: real income per capita has declined in each of the last three years. It can also be seen in the food riots which have recently been reported in the cities of Brazil.

The dilemma facing the international enforcers of "sound finance" is how far the third world countries can be squeezed without provoking social revolutions that will end up in opting out of the imperialist network and possible debt repudiation. But even if such social upheavals can be avoided and enforced depressions should succeed for a time in reducing the balance-of-payments deficits in many third world countries, this will still be a long way from a solution to the crisis. New debt will need to be created to finance even the smaller deficits; and as the total debt keeps piling up, the payment burdens of the debtors will keep on increasing, requiring still more borrowing.

Even at best, therefore, there is no end in sight of the need for continuing third world borrowing. And this raises the question: How much longer can the banks go on supplying the ever-expanding credit to meet this demand? For even though

*Table 4*
*Third World Debt Exposure*
*of the Nine Largest U.S. Banks*

| | *Loans extended ($ billions)* | *Loans as a percent of banks' capital* |
|---|---|---|
| OPEC Members | 16.2 | 71.2 |
| Venezuela | 7.1 | 31.4 |
| Indonesia | 1.9 | 8.4 |
| Saudi Arabia | 1.7 | 7.5 |
| Non-OPEC South American Countries | 40.7 | 178.6 |
| Mexico | 13.6 | 59.8 |
| Brazil | 12.3 | 54.2 |
| Argentina | 5.6 | 24.6 |
| Non-OPEC Asian Countries | 17.3 | 75.9 |
| South Korea | 5.1 | 22.3 |
| Philippines | 3.7 | 16.1 |
| Taiwan | 2.7 | 11.6 |
| Non-OPEC African Countries | 3.6 | 15.7 |
| Total of all underdeveloped countries | 77.7 | 341.4% |

*Source:* Hearing Before the Committee on Banking, Finance, and Urban Affairs, House of Representatives, *International Financial Markets and Related Matters,* Serial No. 97-99, p. 54.

NOTE: The above data are as of June 1982. The nine largest banks and their capital in $ billions—Bank of America (4.1); Citibank (5.1); Chase Manhattan (3.2); Manufacturers Hanover (2.0); Morgan Guaranty (2.3); Continental Illinois (1.8); Chemical Bank (1.6); Bankers Trust (1.4); 1st National Bank of Chicago (1.2). Their total capital is $22.8 billion. Capital consists of the sum of a bank's preferred stock, common stock, surplus, undivided profits, and reserves for contingencies and other capital reserves.

the banks earn hefty profits from their third world involvement (in 1982, 20 percent of Citibank's profits came from Brazil alone), they too are coming up against limits. That can be seen in Table 4. The first column presents the volume of third world loans on the books of the nine largest banks in the United States, as of June 1982. It shows that $77.7 billion of deposits in these banks have been loaned to underdeveloped countries. Now when a bank lends out depositors' money it naturally assumes that the loans will be repaid and that the depositors can therefore have their money back whenever they want it. In the normal course of events some loans will of course go sour, and for this reason contingency reserves are set up. If worse comes to worst, i.e., if contingency reserves prove insufficient, the banks have to dip into accumulated capital to satisfy their depositors. In order to evaluate the exposure of the large banks to third world debt, the loans to these countries need to be expressed as a percentage of the banks' capital (including contingency reserves) as shown in the second column. There we can see, for example, that if Mexico should default on its loans, or declare a unilateral moratorium, almost 60 percent of the capital of the nine banks would be used up to keep the banks in operation. Furthermore, if both Mexico and Brazil should default, the nine banks could be forced out of business, since over 100 percent of their capital would be needed to keep going (at which time a run on the banks would be a distinct possibility). Loans to South American countries (including Venezuela) account for 210 percent of the banks' capital, and loans to the third world as a whole account for over 340 percent.

This is, to be sure, a worst-case scenario. Even such major defaults would not force the banks to close, if the Federal Reserve acted promptly as a lender of last resort to keep them afloat. If the past is a reliable guide, it is reasonable to assume that the Fed would indeed act accordingly. But that is only an assumption, as is the eventuality of default by one or more debtors. Under the circumstances, it is no wonder that fear struck the heart of the financial world when the 1981-82 crisis matured and the number of countries unable to meet their service payments grew. And it is against this background of fear that the banks have become increasingly cautious about extending new loans.

Yet lend they must, for otherwise the debtors would not be able to keep up their contractual payments. The banks count on the IMF as the pillar of the whole system. But the IMF has no solutions either. All it can accomplish is to discipline the debtors and supply short-term funds in dire emergencies. Part of the IMF program is to get the third world countries to import less and export more. Leaving aside the fact that many of them have to import in order to have the supplies to manufacture exports, how can this be a way out if everyone is at the same time reducing imports while trying to increase exports? The upshot of all the frantic rescue measures is hence more of the same: the third world is driven into further debt enslavement and the financial system remains as vulnerable as ever.

The wiser heads in the business community are fully aware that as things stand the problem is insoluble. The schemes they dabble with revolve around either how to get the U.S. public to pay for putting the banks on a sounder basis or how to convert the debt into increased ownership by U.S. capital of third world assets. What none of them are willing to contemplate is the idea that there is nothing sacred about either the profits or the capital of the banks. Why must the banks continue to charge more than nominal interest on the outstanding loans? Why can't the banks' capital be used to write off a portion of the loans? Why not nationalize the banks and do away with them as profit-making institutions?

Sooner or later questions like these will have to be faced and acted on. The alternative possibility is a collapse of the international financial system and with it the opening of a new chapter in the history of the world capitalist system.

# *Third World Debt: Past and Present*

Although today's third world debt crisis has features different from previous crises, it is far from unique in the history of capitalism. Accumulation of foreign debt, with its aftermath of severe financial strains and reduction in the living standards of the people, has long been common to the periphery of the world capitalist system. Conversely, the energetic extension of loans to weaker nations by bankers of the core capitalist nations has long been an important component of Western expansionism, providing stepping stones either to outright colonial occupation or to the kind of economic and political penetration that laid the foundation for, or contributed to, the enduring condition of dependency of peripheral nations on the centers of imperialism.

The record is too long to recite here, but let me note a few examples. In the 1870s the Egyptian government reached a stage of foreign indebtedness so deep that two thirds of its revenue had to be allocated to service the debt. Borrowing abroad was initially undertaken for modernization projects, including the Suez Canal, and to help balance the budget. But the debt obligations piled up as more and more loans were needed just to service past debts. This process continued as long as new loans could be procured. When sources of new funds began to dry up, the Egyptian government could no longer pay the interest owed to foreign bankers and bondholders. This led to the

This article is a reconstruction from notes of a talk by Harry Magdoff given at the Allied Social Science Association meetings, New York City, December 1985. It originally appeared in the February 1986 issue of *Monthly Review*.

steady expansion of intervention by European nations (mainly Britain and France) to take control of Egypt's domestic finances, and eventually provided the excuse for Britain to invade and take over Egypt.

During the nineteenth century, in Tunisia and Morocco (prior to foreign conquest) and in Turkey, Bulgaria, Greece, China, and elsewhere, the threat of default or actual default on foreign debt led to direct control over the finances of these countries by foreign powers—to squeeze out the money to repay the bankers. The history of Latin America is rife with occasions when foreign powers sent gunships to collect customs duties that would be used to pay the foreign creditors. Nor was the United States a laggard on this score: when Britain, Germany, and Italy sent naval ships to blockade Venezuela in order to force debt payments, Washington became alarmed—not because of the principle at stake, but because of the threat of occupation of Venezuela or other Latin American nations by European powers. That prompted Theodore Roosevelt's 1905 declaration of the so-called corollary to the Monroe Doctrine—a warning that the United States might be *compelled* to intervene in the affars of Latin American states in order to remove the grounds for intervention by others. And, as we well know, intervene it did, among other reasons to collect on the debt service owed to U.S. bankers. This happened in, among other places, the Dominican Republic, Haiti, Honduras, Nicaragua, in all of which U.S. representatives took control by military means and enforced treaties involving customs duties—for the sake of the bankers, naturally.*

* The stepped-up flow of loans from stronger to weaker nations was of course an outstanding feature of the new imperialism that emerged in the late nineteenth century. It was, in fact, a key instrument in the intense competition among the leading capitalist powers in their zealous drive to divide the peripheral regions among themselves. An astute student of the subject observed: "The lines of political division in prewar Europe, the situations which were created and which led ultimately to the First World War, can be understood better by taking account of the borrowing-lending relations that existed. On the other hand, the action of capital during this period can be understood better by taking account of the international political influences to which it was subject."(Herbert Feis, *Europe the World's Banker 1870-1914* [New York: W.W. Norton, 1965], p. x.)

Despite this record of continuity, however, there are important differences between the past and the present:

(1) The extension of loans, combined with economic, political, and military pressure, was used in the past to expand capitalism's terrain and bring the noncapitalist nations into the imperialist network. Now, in the era of decolonization and wars of national liberation, the various forms of intervention are designed for the most part to prevent the separation of the peripheral nations from the core—to hinder delinking from the imperialist system.

(2) In the past, the navy and the marines were used to collect the debts. Now, in more sophisticated times and with advanced internationalization of the banks, the International Monetary Fund (IMF) is the main enforcer.

(3) Today, more than in the past, defaults by several large debtor countries have the power to create havoc in the centers of finance.

And yet, despite these differences, certain underlying similarities between then and now prevail:

(1) The extension of loans does more than bring immediate profits to the lenders. It serves also as a door-opener and support for other forms of economic penetration: markets, investment opportunities, acquisition of natural resources.* There is also the symbiotic relation between the bankers and their state: loans are extended as instruments of diplomacy to widen the lending nation's sphere of influence; and the state acts, when needed, directly or through an international agency to assure collection of the debt.

(2) Foreign lending by banks is an important ingredient in the ever persistent drive for more profits. In the 1920s as in the 1970s, representatives could be found sitting at the doorsteps of ministers of finance all over the world, waiting to be received to offer their loans. In effect, they acted as dope push-

* An example of the tie-in between bank loans and acquisition of natural resources is provided by Peru. In the 1870s Peru faced the threat of bankruptcy because of its inability to service its foreign debt. Bankruptcy was avoided by first creating a monopoly of guano operations. The monopoly was then assigned to the French banking firm Dreyfus et Cie., which in return agreed to pay the interest on Peru's foreign debt.

ers. But the process has never been one-sided: the ruling elites of the third world readily became addicts. Consequently, the recent debt expansion led to the familiar dilemma of the inter-war years, when "the great majority of foreign borrowers had been pushed by the U.S. banks' dynamic behavior into a state of indebtedness where new loans were needed just to service the old ones."* And the rationalization behind this development is not new either. Thus in 1928 the accountant general of the Reparations Commission argued:

> The dollar exchange created by the new loans takes care of the old loans and finances new American exports. . . . The expansion, the English tell us, is dangerous to the United States. But I have yet to hear any sensible reasons advanced why it is dangerous and why it cannot go on indefinitely to levels scarcely yet dreamed of. . . . So long as the debtor countries have no export surplus, they will be in the market for new foreign loans, and the debts will be paid by new loans.†

The apprehension here alluded to was typical of the mentality of U.S. bankers before the Great Depression. It was also the mentality of today's bankers before the current crisis set in. Thus in 1977 Citibank published a brochure on *The Emerging Role of Private Banks in the Developing World.* In it there is a list of "canons for lenders." The first canon states: "Do not expect developing countries to be in balance-of-payments surplus on current account over time; assume that current account deficits are normal to such countries." What does this imply other than a constant need on the part of the so-called developing countries to keep on borrowing to cover their ongoing deficits, with ever greater opportunities for the banks to make money by lending to them, with no end in sight?

(3) The picture common throughout the period of imperialism is one in which the peripheral countries are flooded with money when the tide is high and become trapped when the tide ebbs. Equally characteristic, except for those cases in

---

* Marcello de Cecco, "The International Debt Problem in the Interwar Period," in *Banca Nazionale del Lavoro Quarterly Review* (March 1985), p. 59.

** Ibid.

which revolutionary governments have repudiated the debts of the former ruling elites, the ultimate brunt of the debt entrapment has always been borne by the lower classes.

## Inevitability of the Debt Trap

The record of foreign lending and borrowing in the capitalist world reveals two distinct patterns: one where borrowing initially functioned as a vital aid to industrial development, and another where borrowing led to perpetual debt peonage. Outstanding examples of the former are Japan and the United States. In these countries the capitalist class became the dominant component of the ruling elite—a class that imposed the conditions necessary for economic and technological independence and that spread outside its national boundaries to acquire a share of the resources and economic surplus of the globe's underdeveloped areas. Before long debtors of this type became creditors.

Typical of countries that sank into unending debt were those that were colonized or became informal outposts of empire. There the long history of colonialism and economic penetration resulted in one-sided distorted socioeconomic formations. As a rule, the landed aristocrats retained control over tillable land as well as a good deal of political power, enabling them to stand in the way of the kind of agricultural revolution that has always been the precondition of successful capitalism. In these countries the patterns of economic growth—in natural resource extraction, industry, and foreign trade—were and continue to be determined by foreign investment and loans. The emerging business community in this environment was one that fitted into the new patterns, and accordingly lacked the motive or strength to struggle for economic independence. This kind of capitalist class works in tandem with foreign investors and bankers for the sake of its own prosperity, and relies on cooperation with the landed aristocracy to keep the impoverished masses in hand. Because of the high degree of dependency on the technology, markets, and investment of the advanced capitalist countries, there is frequent recourse to borrowing abroad. And that in turn reinforces the dependent relationship.

There is furthermore an innate logic to debt reliance that leads directly into the trap. This can be seen from a simple arithmetical exercise. Let us assume that a country borrows $1,000 every year under terms that call for repayment in 20 years in equal installments, plus 10 percent interest on the outstanding balance. As the debt accumulates from year to year so does the amount that must be sent back to the bankers. If we follow through with the arithmetic we find that in the fifth year the bill for interest and amortization on past debt amounts to $700. Hence, of the $1,000 borrowed in that year only $300 is left over for other needs. By the eighth year and thereafter the annual $1,000 loan is no longer sufficient to service the past debt: the need to borrow keeps on growing. And that is in the nature of the case. Barring a drastic change in the country's situation, borrowing has to continue and even *increase* if only to keep up payments to the banks.*

Debt, however, is only one claw in the dependency trap. As we have seen, debt produces the need for still more debt. But so do other aspects of the ties between the periphery and the metropole. This is vividly demonstrated by what lies behind the persistent balance-of-payments difficulties in the third world. Recall Citibank's dictum to bankers about the underdeveloped nations: "Assume that current account deficits are normal to such countries." To see why this is so let us look at the data on the current balance-of-payments for all of Latin America (except Cuba) in 1982, the year when the crisis broke out in full force.

A few words of explanation are needed before we present the data. The overall balance of payments is a summary of all the financial transactions between a country and the rest of the world. There are two parts to it: a balance on current account and a balance on capital account. The former totals the day-to-day transactions (purchases and sales of goods and services), while the latter encompasses the longer term money movements

---

* The illustration discussed here is presented in fuller detail in "The Two Faces of Third World Debt," this volume, pp. 176-85; and a demonstration of how this applies to the case of Mexico can be found in John C. Pool and Stephen C. Stamos, "The Uneasy Calm: Third World Debt—The Case of Mexico," MR, March 1985.

(capital investment and loans). In general, what is owing in the former category has to be settled fairly promptly if trade and service transactions are to be sustained on an ongoing basis. Thus if there is a deficit on current account, borrowing abroad or attracting capital investment is necessary to avoid economic disruption or bankruptcy. The crucial area to examine for the purpose at hand is thus the behavior of the current-account balance.

Now let us look at the data. For the sake of simplification, the accompanying table summarizes the multitude of current account transactions in four categories. The first line of the table shows the balance between exports and imports of goods. The next gives the net figure on outlays for freight and insurance. After that comes the net payment to foreigners for interest, dividends, royalties, and management fees. The remaining category is a catchall combining thousands of transactions, as, for example, travel costs, tourist expenditures, harbor and airport fees, etc.

*Table 1*
*Balance of Payments on Current Account: Latin America (except Cuba), 1982*

| *Balance on* | *Billions of dollars* |
|---|---|
| Merchandise trade | + 7.1 |
| Freight and insurance | – 2.7 |
| Investment | –37.1 |
| All other items | – 7.6 |
| Total | –40.3 |

Source: Inter-American Development Bank, *Economic and Social Progress in Latin America, 1984 Report.*

When all four categories are combined we find that in 1982 Latin American countries as a whole had a whopping *deficit* of over $40 billion on current account. And the reason for this is crystal clear. As can be seen from the table, exports of merchandise exceeded imports by $7.1 billion. On the other hand, "all other items" show a deficit of $7.6 billion. It follows that if nothing else were involved, there would have been an unimportant minuscule deficit. The trouble comes from the middle two items. Merchandise was shipped mainly in foreign-owned bottoms and the transportation was insured by firms in the financial centers, leading to an outflow of $2.7 billion. That in itself is a product of the whole history of dependency, but it is still a small part of the problem. The real squeeze arises from the outflow of $37.1 billion on investment account. About half of that (over $18 billion) went to bankers and bondholders for interest due on past debt and the rest wound up mainly in the coffers of industrial corporations.*

In short, the reason for the deficit is the tribute to foreign capital—for shipping, insurance, interest, and various forms of profit. Within the market system, the debtor countries cover their deficits by attracting more foreign investment or borrowing from international bankers, the IMF, and the World Bank. But all that does is to intensify the problem, since still more is going to have to be paid abroad for interest and profits. Therein lies the trap of debt peonage.

## Third World Societies and the Debt Trap

A con game has two sides: those who do the conning and those who are conned. Those who are conned are often innocent, naive people who are easily duped. But more typically they are willing and active participants. That is surely the case as far as the elites of the third world are concerned, for the ruling groups in those countries benefit directly and indirectly from the economic ties with the advanced capitalist nations. What is even more significant is that the upper crusts of these societies are ardent advocates of the free market and the free flow of money across borders. They seek the freedom not only to get money from abroad but also to ship their profits to other lands. And, indeed, the third world wealthy have for years been shifting vast sums to bank deposits, real estate operations, enterprises, and securities in the United States and Western Europe. This has been going on even at the height of the debt

* That this overall picture is typical and not a chance occurrence in 1982 can be seen from the data given for earlier years in the Review of the Month, "International Economic Distress and the Third World," MR, April 1982, and in Two Faces of Third World Debt," this volume, pp. 176-85.

crisis. World Bank estimates show a capital flight of approximately $67 billion from Mexico, Venezuela, and Argentina during 1979-82, and there is good reason to believe that there has been no letup of such flight from these countries and others since 1982.*

David Felix, professor of economics at Washington University in St. Louis, tackled this issue in a provocative article in the November/December 1985 issue of *Challenge.* Pulling together information from several sources, he reaches the conclusion that wealthy Latin Americans have salted away at least $180 billion outside their continent. That amounts to half the region's current foreign debt! Yet wages and budgets are slashed while the capital flight goes on. Nor is there any interest in, or even discussion of, recapturing these assets to reduce foreign debts. Some may argue that such action would interfere with capitalist property rights. But that is exactly what the advanced capitalist states have done in times of emergency, as pointed out by Felix:

> Coercive mobilization . . . was used in the past by major capitalist countries in duress. During World War I, Britain and France, the two leading international lenders of the laissez-faire era, compelled their nationals to register their foreign securities with the Treasury, which liquidated them as needed, paying the owners in local currency bonds, the foreign exchange being used to help cover current account deficits. As the Chancellor of the Exchequer put it to Parliament, "The government wanted to get these securities, as far as possible, into one hand, so that they might be controlled and used for the purpose of paying our debts in the United States. They believed that these securities would afford us a very great resource which would be fully sufficient to meet our liabilities."
>
> With the World War experience in mind, the Tory government on the eve of World War II took the precaution of requiring registration of all foreign securities, which could sell them as needed, and did. (pp. 50-51)

Why was this possible in strong capitalist nations and not even on the agenda of the peripheral countries? Why are the people being squeezed unconscionably while private capital is

* *Wall Street Journal*, 11 October 1985.

allowed to flee to "safe and profitable havens"? A full answer would require a more extensive and complex analysis than can be undertaken here. We believe, however, that the crux of the matter is the nature of the dependency relationship to the center and the accommodating unstable class alliances that govern the underdeveloped societies. For the same reasons, repudiation of the debt and nationalization of foreign investment are not seen as a possible way out of the debt trap. Such drastic moves would necessitate a radical redirection of the economy toward self-reliance, and that would not be possible without a major transfer of power from the dominant classes whose interests are identified with the existing international social structure.

# *Questions for the Peace Movement*

Gorbachev's proposal to eliminate nuclear weapons by the year 2000—published in full in an ad paid for by the Soviet Embassy in the *New York Times* of February 4th—raises, directly and indirectly, a whole series of questions of vital concern to the U.S. peace movement, of which we of course consider ourselves to be a part. In what follows we try to identify some of the more important of these questions and to provide at least tentative answers in a form suitable for discussion and debate.

First, is elimination of nuclear weapons the main goal of the peace movement? And would its achievement lay the basis for a lasting peace?

The answer has to be no to both these questions. There were wars long before there were nuclear weapons, and wars have been going on continuously since August 6, 1945, without the use of nuclear weapons. Obviously there could be wars, even wars of unprecedented destructiveness, even if no one possessed nuclear weapons.

What, then, is the importance of the elimination issue? At least for a time, and perhaps a long time, it would vastly reduce the twin dangers of nuclear war and the annihilation of the human race, and this would of course be an extremely important and enormously encouraging achievement. However, it is important to understand that even total elimination would not do away with these dangers. Knowledge of how to produce nuclear weapons exists, and it is most unlikely to be lost or forgotten. If a war involving advanced industrial powers were to break out after the elimination of nuclear weapons, all contending parties

---

This article originally appeared in the March 1986 issue of *Monthly Review*.

would almost certainly begin manufacturing them again, even if only to be able to deter their use by others. In other words, the world would be back to square one. It is thus obvious that the search for peace involves much more than the elimination of nuclear weapons (or any other types or combination of types of weapons). What needs to be eliminated is whatever it is that motivates nations to resort to war against each other.

Pinning this down must therefore be the first step on the way to defining the tasks of the peace movement. But we cannot expect to be able to give a *general* answer to the question of the causes of war, nor of course can we accept at face value what the participants tell us about the causes of specific wars. Throughout history wars have been waged for many reasons, and it is no exaggeration to say that one of the most important tasks of historians has always been to try to figure out what were the real, as distinct from the proclaimed, causes of particular wars.

If this much is accepted, it follows that the first obligations of a peace movement ought to be (1) to study history in depth with a view to learning how to analyze past wars and their causes, and (2) to use the knowledge thus gained to examine wars recently concluded, now going on, or likely to break out in the foreseeable future.

As already noted, we cannot accept at face value what the participants tell us. Nowadays, it is standard operating procedure for everyone concerned to claim self-defense—there are no War Departments any more, only Defense Departments—and it goes without saying that there are cases in which the claim is valid. The period leading up to and culminating in the Second World War was full of them, and it is important not to forget it. But we have to consider every case on its merits, and it is always wise to approach the task without preconceived conclusions.

Against this background we can turn to the preoccupations of the peace movement in this country in the here and now.

The first thing that strikes us and that needs to be focused on is the simple fact that the United States is engaged on an unprecedented peacetime military build-up. The budget submitted by President Reagan for fiscal year 1987 as we write these lines calls for military spending of $274.3 billion, amounting to about 28 percent of total outlays. Why?

Some may argue that this is a piece of Reaganite insanity, to be rectified as soon as the present bunch of crazies is out of office. The trouble with this argument is that the present build-up (from an already high level) began under the (relatively) liberal Carter administration; and, with very few exceptions, the Democrats in Congress are asking for no more than marginal reductions in Reagan's proposal, and that for fiscal not military reasons. Clearly, it will not do to treat the Reagan administration's military policies as an aberration: basically they are of a piece with those of earlier administrations and must be considered bipartisan national policies. Unless this fact is recognized and explained, there is little likelihood of developing a coherent and ultimately successful peace movement.

Ask a representative sample of U.S. citizens why they support, or at least do not oppose, the military build-up and they will probably tell you we have to be strong to counter potential Russian aggression. Probe a bit further, however, and you will find that very few if any believe the Russians have the intention, the means, or the stupidity to attack this country. So why the need for a monstrous military build-up?

Here we reach the heart of the matter: anti-Communism, which in geopolitical terms translates into a belief in the implacable expansionism of the Soviet Union. This idea has been assiduously propagated and drilled into the minds of the American people ever since the Russian Revolution of 1917 by all the cultural and ideological institutions and organs under the control of perhaps the strongest and most firmly entrenched hegemonic ruling class that history has ever known. Most Americans undoubtedly believe it, and even those who are skeptical are quite likely to accept it as a worst-case scenario to be taken seriously in the formulation of foreign policy. The small minority who reject it as not only unfounded but in flat contradiction to the weight of the historical evidence have been and continue to be excluded from the forum of discussion and debate in which public opinion is formed.

To understand what acceptance of the belief in the stark reality of Soviet expansionism implies for the peace movement, we must transport ourselves back to the 1930s when Hitler came to power in Germany, having already proclaimed in *Mein Kampf* his goal of world conquest. Many people of course didn't believe he was serious. They reasoned that Germany had legitimate grievances stemming from the peace treaty forced on her at the end of the First World War, and that Hitler's bellicosity would subside if concessions were made to Germany's demands for revision of the treaty. This view, summed up in the term "appeasement" and superimposed on a strong current of pacifism arising from the horrible slaughter of the recent war, put its stamp on what was probably the most numerous segment of the international peace movement of the period. But there was another wing of the peace movement which took Hitler seriously, not because it regarded him as trustworthy but because it understood well the nature of German imperialism and the impasse into which it had been driven by defeat in the imperialist war and Germany's consequent demotion to a position in the international hierarchy of power far below its relatively undiminished economic potential. Those who took this view included most of the left, in which at the time the Soviet Union and its partisans in the international Communist movement constituted the largest element.

What actually happened of course totally discredited the "appeasers" and vindicated the views of those who believed that Hitler could be stopped and the Second World War prevented only by confronting Germany with an overwhelmingly powerful alliance of opposing military forces. The lesson was learned the hard way, by six more years of bloodshed and destruction, and it certainly has not been forgotten in the forty years that have intervened since the end of the Second World War.

The crucial question now facing the peace movement is whether this lesson is applicable to the situation in which the world finds itself today.

The right says yes, and it backs up the claim by the simple and, we must admit, extremely effective device of substituting Soviet Russia for Nazi Germany. Once it is accepted that this is legitimate, i.e., that the Soviet Union, like Germany a half century earlier, is bent on world conquest, everything else follows. Hitler was a liar and a cheat; his protestations of peaceful intent were but a prelude to fresh aggressions; appeasement only convinced him of the weakness of his intended victims; the *only* way to stop him was to confront him with overwhelmingly superior power. This his opponents failed to do, with results the world has lived to regret ever since. This is the lesson the right applies to the situation that exists today, with one important addition: failure to stop the aggressor in the nuclear age could, and probably would, mean that we would never again have even the luxury of regret.

At first sight it may appear that acceptance of this view can at best condemn the world to an open-ended period of confrontation between two superpower-led blocs armed to the teeth with every kind of weapon from guns and tanks to nuclear bombs and Star Wars and god knows what horrors the scientists and technologists of the future may dream up. Some who accept the underlying logic of this position may consider it the only kind of peace we can hope for in the foreseeable future—even if, as they can hardly deny, it clearly implies the slow death of civilization as we have known it. But this is not the way the most serious—and probably the most influential—ideologists of the right see matters. They believe that the arms race is not only the way to contain Soviet aggression but also the way to put so much pressure on the Soviet socioeconomic system that it will eventually be literally forced to give up the struggle and accept a position subordinate to the United States (and its economically powerful allies) in the global power structure. This would imply, though not necessarily immediately, the restoration of capitalism in the Soviet Union and other postrevolutionary societies that have managed to break free of the regime of capital (using that term in the sense analyzed in this space in last month's issue of MR). Even the most optimistic right-wing theorists do not imagine that "winning" the arms race in this way would solve all the problems of war and peace, but they do believe that the nature of these problems would change in a fundamental way, and to this we would have to agree.

There is, however, no point in pursuing the analysis of this scenario further. It needs only to be refuted and rejected. The great Columbia Nobel prize-winning physicist I. Rabi was recently quoted on a TV talk show as saying that if the Soviet Union could recover from the indescribable losses of human and material resources inflicted by the Second World War and in a few years' time rise to the undisputed position of one of the world's two superpowers, it could certainly sustain any level of arms build-up as well as the United States (he might have said, even better). Wishful thinking has always led the right to overestimate the inner strength of capitalism and underestimate that of the post-revolutionary societies. No, there is no victory of any kind for anyone at the end of the arms race.

But this is not all that needs to be refuted. The whole complex of assumptions on which the arms race is based is as flawed as the notion of winning the arms race. The Soviet Union is not Nazi Germany, and the 1980s are not the 1930s. Let us consider these statements in turn.

First, while the history of Nazi Germany records an almost non-stop string of aggressions practically from the day Hitler came to power, that of the Soviet Union is entirely different and indeed very close to the exact opposite. More than a half dozen capitalist countries, including the United States, invaded Russia in 1918-20; the United States refused even to recognize the existence of the Soviet regime until 1933; Japan launched large-scale attacks against the Soviet far east in the late 1920s and 1930s; the officially labeled "Anti-Communist" German-Italian-Japanese Axis was formed in 1936; Hitler launched his all-out invasion of the USSR in 1941; and the alliance between the West and the Soviet Union that resulted in the defeat of Germany and Japan in the Second World War was followed almost immediately by the U.S. reversion to an obsessive anti-Communism which has been the *leitmotiv* of every postwar administration from Truman to Reagan. The Soviet Union has naturally tried to defend itself in every way available to it, including installing satellite regimes on its borders—the counterpart of the *cordon sanitaire* established by the Versailles Treaty around revolutionary Russia after the First World War—and bolstering them up by economic, political, and when necessary military means. It is the instances in which the Soviet Union felt it necessary to intervene militarily (particularly Hungary, Czechoslovakia, and Afghanistan) that are held up as examples of Soviet expansionism. The case for this interpretation, when viewed in the context of the broad sweep of twentieth-century history, is pitifully weak. And when seen, as it must be, as the ultimate rationale for the present U.S. military build-up, it can only be characterized as positively ludicrous.

But this is not all. The whole international scene in the 1980s is radically different from that of the 1930s. In those days there really was a mad-dog imperialism on the loose, thirsting for revenge for its defeat and territorial losses in the First World War and harboring unlimited expansionist ambitions. Nothing of the kind exists today.

The United States, the big victor in the Second World War, is a sated imperialist power if ever there was one. Its ambition is not to conquer the world but rather: (1) to hold onto the hegemonic position in the capitalist part of the world it acquired, as it were by default, in the Second World War; and (2) to prevent this capitalist part of the world from shrinking through revolutionary defections. Post-Second World War history has shown that both of these aims are highly elusive. Economically, if not militarily, U.S. hegemony is being increasingly challenged by other capitalist powers; and not only have revolutionary defections occurred in various parts of the third world but the conditions that gave rise to them are ripening everywhere. Under these circumstances, the very idea of the United States as an expanding imperialist power is a hopeless anachronism.

The Soviet Union for its part is also a satisfied power. It was the other big winner of the Second World War and with some exceptions (Austria, North Korea) it held on directly or indirectly to territories occupied by its armies during the war; in terms of resources it is largely self-sufficient; and its most vulnerable borders are adequately buffered.* Though heir to most of the territorial acquisitions of Tsarist expansionism, the

* Afghanistan is an exception here. But there are indications that negotiations being conducted under the auspices of the United Nations could, if the Reagan administration is willing to cooperate, lead to a fairly early Soviet withdrawal and an overall settlement acceptable to regionally interested nations.

Soviet Union broke sharply with that tradition under Lenin after the First World War and in the realm of ideology continues to adhere to the classical anti-imperialist tenets of Marxist doctrine.

A sober analysis of today's international situation thus leads to the conclusion that neither of the superpowers, and still less any of the lesser powers, is aggressively expansionist in the sense that most major powers were before the First World War and the Axis powers were in the period between the world wars.

This situation leads to the conclusion that the real danger of war today is entirely different from that which led to the Second World War (or the First World War either for that matter). To identify *this* danger, not that which preceded the earlier wars of this century, is therefore the number one responsibility of the peace movement of the 1980s. It can hardly be overemphasized that it is a *new* danger and one that the peace movement has for the most part not yet even recognized, let alone adequately analyzed.

This does not mean that the widespread impression that the world faces a war crisis is wrong. What it does mean is that this war crisis is the distorted reflection of another, far more complex crisis that has been building up for decades and shows no signs of abating in the visible future. It is this underlying crisis that ineluctably generates tensions, both internationally and within countries, and threatens sooner or later to explode in a general conflagration.

This underlying crisis is the growing failure of capitalism, the social system that embraces some two thirds of the earth's territory and population, to solve the elementary and, in the long run, the very survival requirements of the vast majority of those living under its sway.

In saying this, we are not advancing or reviving an idea which was once adhered to by some elements of the international socialist movement, i.e., that capitalism must eventually experience a catastrophic crisis of a kind that would render its further existence impossible. The concept of such a final breakdown of the system was never entertained by Marx and in fact makes no sense. Societies are not like organisms that die or machines that cease to function; they continue to exist and function unless and until they are replaced by other societies.

Further, we are not even saying or implying that capitalism, judged by its own standards, is in some sort of irreversible decline. The crisis of capitalism we are talking about is not new, and the system's ideologists and protagonists for the most part do not conceive it as a crisis at all. Its origins go back a long way—in a sense back to the origins of the system itself—but it was not until after the Second World War that it began to acquire the character of the world-dominating force it now is. And most of this period, at least up to the mid-1970s, was one of unparalleled capitalist expansion as measured by such conventional indexes as GNP, volume of trade, average per capita income, etc. The performance of the past decade has been less impressive, but there is no reason to assume that the slowdown is necessarily permanent. Even if those who anticipate another long wave of expansion should turn out to be right, the underlying crisis of the system would in no way be mitigated: in fact quite the contrary.

What, then, is the nature of this underlying crisis?

It has two facets. First is the working out, through upswings and downswings and with ever more dire consequences, of what Marx called "the absolute general law of capitalist accumuation":

> The greater the social wealth, the functioning capital, the extent and energy of its growth, and therefore also the absolute mass of the proletariat and the productiveness of its labor, the greater is the industrial reserve army. . . . But the greater this reserve army in proportion to the active labor army, the greater is the mass of a consolidated surplus population, whose misery is in inverse ratio to its torment of labor. The more extensive, finally, the lazarus-layers of the working class and the industrial reserve army, the greater is official pauperism. *This is the absolute general law of capitalist accumulation.* (*Capital,* Vol. 1, Ch. XXIII, Sect. 4, emphasis in the original)

Nowadays of course the field of action of this "law" is the entire global capitalist system, and its most spectacular manifestations are in the third world where unemployment rates range up to 50 percent and destitution, hunger, and starvation are increasingly endemic. But the advanced capitalist nations are by no means immune to its operation: more than 30 million men and women, in excess of 10 percent of the available labor force, are unemployed in the OECD countries; and in the United States itself, the richest of them all, officially defined poverty rates are rising even in a period of cyclical upswing.

The second facet of the underlying capitalist crisis is the unprecedented scale and speed of the deterioration of the natural environment within which human society must perforce exist and to which it must ultimately either adapt or perish. Here again the third world is the scene of the most significant developments. Quantitative measures are harder to come by in ecological than in economic affairs. But reliable studies, still all too scarce and incomplete, leave no doubt about what is happening and what lies ahead if no effective corrective action is taken. Readers unfamiliar with such studies should pay careful attention to the review in this issue of MR of two recent reports on the ecological scene in India, the most populous country in the world capitalist system (M. R. Bhagavan, "Halting India's Environmental Devastation"). The evidence contained in these reports, as summarized by Bhagavan, is no less dramatic and alarming for being presented in the low-key language of serious scholarship. Nor is there any reason to assume that among third world countries India is an untypical case.

The underlying crisis of capitalism, then, is an appalling and, by historical standards, extremely rapid deterioration in the conditions of existence of a clear and growing majority of humankind.

It is true that, with relatively few exceptions, people in the advanced capitalist countries are not even aware of the existence of this crisis. Media reporting and comment usually focus on the short run, emphasizing cyclical phenomena and drawing optimistic or pessimistic conclusions according to the conditions of the moment. Speculation about the longer run is common enough and often takes sensational forms, but it is always treated as essentially irrelevant to the present. Prestigious figures looked upon as reliable sources of understanding and wisdom can be counted on to end up with comforting reassurances about the future. Typical—and particularly relevant in the present context—is the view recently expressed by Secretary of State George Shultz, formerly head of a major U.S. corporation and before that Dean of the University of Chicago Business School. Referring to a long history of "fashionable Marxist mythology" concerning an alleged crisis of capitalism, Shultz wrote:

> They were wrong. Today—in a supreme irony—it is the Communist system that looks bankrupt, morally as well as economically. The West [i.e., capitalism] is resilient and resurgent.
>
> And so, in the end, the most important new way of thinking that is called for in this decade is our way of thinking about ourselves. Civilizations thrive when they believe in themselves. ("Shaping American Foreign Policy: New Realities and New Ways of Thinking," *Foreign Affairs,* Spring 1985)

But the people who bear the brunt of today's far-from-mythological crisis of capitalism—the dispossessed and destitute masses of the third world—can hardly be expected to share Mr. Shultz's enthusiasm for the "resilience and resurgence" of the system that oppresses them. Events of the past half century—the Second World War, the dismantling of the old colonial empires, successful revolutions in various parts of the world—have given them a new awareness of the possibility of change, while a long string of broken promises of reform and help from the wealthy metropolises has taught them not to rely on salvation from outside. More and more their sights are set on genuine national liberation and profound structural change, increasingly perceived as achievable only through taking control of their own destinies. Not that outside help is spurned—quite the contrary. But it must be on their own terms, not on those of the donors.

On the face of it, this situation does not seem necessarily to contain the danger of a new war. Practically every nation state in the world owes its present social structure and form of government to a revolution at some time in the past; and most of the revolutions of the twentieth century have come after—and at least been partly caused by—wars rather than preceding and playing a part in causing them. If the third world, or at least an important part of it, is in revolutionary ferment, why should that be either a surprise to any well informed person or a reason for military confrontations between major military powers?

The answer, unfortunately, is all too clear: the United States has in effect proclaimed to the whole world that the guiding principle of its international policy is total opposition to any revolution anywhere, and that it is prepared to use any and all means available to it, including nuclear weapons, to implement this commitment to global counter-revolution. That this stance does indeed contain a threat of new wars is not a matter of speculation: beginning with Greece during the Second World War, the United States has repeatedly intervened militarily, both covertly and overtly, to block revolutionary change in third world countries.* And twice—in Korea and Vietnam—the result has been a major regional war which in both cases came close at times to expanding into a much wider conflict. There is a tendency today to forget that a significant escalation did in fact take place in the Korean war when China intervened to keep U.S. forces from establishing themselves on the Chinese border; and that if MacArthur had had his way, a full-fledged war against China would have been all but inevitable—at a time, moreover, when the Chinese-Soviet alliance was in full force.

As to the future it is easy to imagine a scenario—originating, say, in a revolution in India—which would bring the United States and the Soviet Union into direct confrontation. Those who believe that the U.S. policy of global counter-revolution bears within it no danger of a Third World War are simply out of touch with historical facts and present realities.

Of course the policy of global counterrevolution is not presented as such by spokespeople, official or otherwise, for the U.S. ruling establishment. Oh no, it is a glorious crusade for democracy and a selfless struggle to save the world from the evil empire of Communism. If you don't believe it, just read the newspapers and listen to the television reports in these closing days of February when our former colony, the Philippines, occupies center stage in this titanic battle between good and evil.

* In several cases, "mildly reformist" or at most "potentially revolutionary" would be a more accurate description, but this only goes to show the extreme sensitivity of U.S. policy to any perceived threat to the status quo from the left.

What a monumental farce! There can't be anything remotely resembling real democracy in the Philippines unless and until one of the world's rottenest and most corrupt ruling classes, long maintained in power by U.S. economic and military support, has been overthrown by a popular revolution and the Philippine people have installed a government representing their own interests rather than the interests of their domestic and foreign exploiters.* And who is fighting for just such a revolution? The evil ones of course, the New Peoples Army and its supporters who include Communists, a large part of the country's Catholics, and increasingly the rural masses who have historically produced the bulk of the nation's wealth and received in return barely enough to keep alive in what could be a flourishing land.

If the analysis presented in this essay is accepted, a conclusion of overwhelming importance to the peace movement logically follows: without a truly fundamental change in U.S. foreign policy, there can be no progress toward ridding the world of the war danger that now hangs over humankind like a sword of Damocles. Anti-Communism is a fool's game. It poisons the mind and generates policies that are quite literally suicidal. There are those in the peace movement who understand this, though unfortunately most of them remain silent for fear of scaring off the millions who have been brain-washed into believing that Communism is their deadly enemy. The time has come, we believe, for them to ask themselves whether there is any hope of being able to build an effective peace movement if it is afraid to tell the truth about the real danger of war.

---

* Since this was written, the Marcos dictatorship has collapsed, Marcos himself has gone into exile, and Corazon Aquino has assumed the presidency of the country. These are of course welcome developments, but their significance should not be exaggerated. The new situation may well lead to the relaxation of the fascist-type repression of the Marcos period, and this would create, at least for a time, conditions much more favorable for the political organization and activity of workers, peasants, and the marginalized population of the shanty towns. But it would be hopelessly naive to expect any basic changes to result from the reshuffling of personnel at the top levels of government.